ESSENTIAL AFRICAN MYTHOLOGY

In *the same series*:

Essential Celtic Mythology
Lindsay Clarke

Essential Russian Mythology
Pyotr Simonov

Essential Chinese Mythology
Martin Palmer and Zhao Xiaomin

Essential African Mythology

STORIES THAT CHANGE THE WORLD

NGANGAR MBITU AND RANCHOR PRIME

Thorsons
An Imprint of HarperCollinsPublishers

For Anna, Thalia and Sava

Thorsons
An Imprint of HarperCollins*Publishers*
77–85 Fulham Palace Road,
Hammersmith, London W6 8JB
1160 Battery Street
San Francisco, California 94111–1213

Published by Thorsons 1997

1 3 5 7 9 10 8 6 4 2

©Ngangar Mbitu and Ranchor Prime 1997

Ngangar Mbitu and Ranchor Prime assert the moral
right to be identified as the authors of this work
A catalogue record for this book
is available from the British Library

ISBN 1 85538 478 7

Printed in Great Britain by
Caledonian International Book Manufacturing Ltd, Glasgow

All rights reserved. No part of this publication may be
reproduced, stored in a retrieval system, or transmitted,
in any form or by any means, electronic, mechanical,
photocopying, recording or otherwise, without the prior
permission of the publishers.

Contents

Introduction vii

Chapter One Myths of Origin and Extinction 1

Chapter Two The Elements and Celestial Powers 58

Chapter Three Gods and Spirits 77

Chapter Four Animals and Humans 93

Chapter Five Folk Stories 116

Chapter Six Fables 149

Resources 177

Anthologies 179

Introduction

Generally speaking, African myths may be understood as imaginative traditions not only about the nature, history and destiny of the world, but also about the gods, humanity and society. As stories representing cultural emblems, they are of considerable interest and importance since they touch on the most fundamental issues of life. According to Jan Knappert, each ethnic or tribal group in Africa has its own unique set of religious beliefs. Naturally, there are certain recognizable similarities from place to place, but variation is more the rule than the exception. The most frequent areas of agreement occur where neighbouring tribes or villages speak related languages. For, on the African continent, particularly south of the Sahara, linguistic relationship is both a sign of common history among different peoples and a sign of shared elements in their mythological traditions.

Today, however, most of the traditional African religions have virtually ceased to exist. Whether by commitment or by coercion, the majority of Africans have accepted either Islam (especially in north and west Africa, the Sudan and Somalia) or Christianity (in most of central or southern Africa). Of the very few nations that have maintained a particularly strong culture-consciousness, there are the Yoruba in Nigeria, the Fon of Benin, the Ashanti in Ghana, and a few tribes in the Sudan, who have been resilient to change and have managed to preserve their old beliefs and pantheons. As for the ancient traditions themselves, the only picture that is available must be derived from archival records and surviving orally-transmitted accounts. While much of African mythology is religious in nature, in that the tales convey sacred truths, not all myths are of necessity religious, as this collection clearly reveals. Some may be primarily social and historical: even the gods may play somewhat secondary or inferior roles in them, sometimes no role at all. The function of this kind of myth (principally the ones listed under 'Animals and Humans, Folk Stories' and 'Fables' in this anthology) is to clarify the history and rationale of a social group, institution, tradition, custom or social development. A myth which relates the tale of a people, for example, supports their sense of solidarity and purpose, of confidence and pride in themselves.

Inevitably, old myths have been lost, but new ones, reflecting and fulfilling changed cultural circumstances, are born from the thesaurus of motives, themes and subjects that have been inherited from the past. Because of their very nature, and as a reflection of developing social circumstances, myths flourish for a time and then fade and die out. The new myths may be hybrid forms, a merging of new and old, or a mingling with neighbouring traditions. Nevertheless, the African myths stand as genuine narratives or traditional tales which enshrine a fundamental truth about the world and human life. They are seen as authoritative and fundamental to the most deep-seated traditions of any group or community.

One class of myths identifies social habits, such as hunting, fishing or tilling the earth. These stories give the community the sense of sharing in the existence of their forefathers through continuing their way of life. Another class justifies the regulations of social order: institutions, cultic behaviour, community stratification, laws, customs, ethical standards, values and ideas. To this

Introduction

group belong tales of kinship, marriage customs, cultural activities, husbandry, hunting, fishing and warfare, along with numerous other features of a society's fabric. Occasionally, these narratives play an important moral function in defining appropriate and inappropriate behaviour.

In addition to the myths that are linked closely with ceremony, custom and ritual, a large number also deal with issues and concerns of human existence. The narratives in this book demonstrate how the Africans attempted to unravel the meaning of existence, the origin of creation: animals, plants and humans; the distinction between the two sexes; the discovery of fire; the beginning of social order; the reason for disease, old age; and the inevitability of death.

Africa is one of the largest of the land masses on this planet. It occupies over thirty million square kilometres; it is three times larger than Europe and covers nearly a quarter of the total territory of the earth. A lot of this land is desert and wilderness, peopled by nomads who for centuries have learned how to survive in what the modern world would describe as hostile conditions. The Sahara is the fiercest of the continent's deserts. Covering over sixteen million square kilometres, it is a vast and inhospitable ocean of sand. But there are also other equally formidable stretches of sand, such as the Kalahari, Namib, Nubian, Turkana, and Somali deserts.

In Central Africa, which comprises Zaire, Uganda, the Congo, Gabon and Cameroon, the sandy wastes give way to rich tropical forests – the home of such exotic creatures as the pygmy hippopotamus, the okapi, the gorilla, the chimp, the leopard, the pygmy antelope, the Congo peacock and the red buffalo. In addition to these, there are innumerable species of birds, reptiles and fish. The rest of the continent is made up of the savannah, a grassy plain, sometimes flat, sometimes undulating, sometimes swampy, mostly dry and dusty. The savannah stretches from Gambia and Senegal in the west across the Central African Republic to Kenya. From there it reaches all the way down to South Africa where it is called the veldt.

Many animals and birds also inhabit the savannah and like the beasts of the tropical forests, these frequently occupy significant roles in African myths and legends. Certain animals have been given stereotyped characteristics: the proud and lazy lion, the wise, silent giraffe, the cunning toad, the deceitful tortoise, the lazy chameleon, the efficient lizard (see, for example, *The Dog and the Toad* and *The Chameleon and the Lizard* and the Tortoise stories under *Fables*). Every animal is given its own personality, essentially the traits of humans, for in the myths the beasts are men and women in another guise.

Most nations in the sub-Saharan continent acknowledge the existence of a Supreme Being – a 'high' or 'sky' god, occasionally associated with thunder and lightning. Also found in the African pantheon are the earth, the sun, the moon and the sea gods. Among the western tribes in particular the mysterious and elusive forest god is prominent. After all, the forest contains almost everything needed for human survival: fruit, game, wood for burning and for making tools and furniture, bark for clothes, leaves for vegetables, lianas for rope and for snares, roots and juices for medicine and strong drink. Hence, a number of African tribes look on the forest as the dwelling of deities, or the domain of spirits, so that anyone wishing to enter it has to take special precautions (this is well illustrated in *Kigbo and the Bush Spirits*) and to perform certain rituals.

Several of the older myths present characters that are animals or insects with fabulous powers. The spider, for example, can spin a web that reaches from earth to heaven (see *A Daughter-in-law for Kimanaweze*), the antelope can climb up to the moon (see *Antelope in the Moon*) and an entire civilization can live and work inside a fish (see *Chichinguane and Chipfalamfula*). Even the stretching python can reach from horizon to horizon. In time, animals may transform into half-human, half-beast characters that can be either evil demons or good spirits. Sometimes the dividing line between humans and animals is completely blurred, as shown in *The Hunter and the Hind*. If these beings marry ordinary mortals, they can give birth to human children. For this reason many clans claim descent from animal ancestors who become their 'totems' or symbols (see, for example, *The Boy and the Leopard* and *Tortoise and Babarinsa's Daughters*).

Gods and Lesser Deities

The distinction between gods and spirits is somewhat arbitrary although, generally speaking, the gods are more powerful than the spirits and their characters are more fully developed. Many African peoples believed that everything in nature, human and non-human alike, had a spirit, some of which were mighty and powerful, like the strong-willed mind of a great warrior chief (such as *Chief Liongo*) or of a killer beast (such as *The Sheep God*). At times, even tree spirits could prove to be both mighty and wise, such as the one in *The Sheep God* that imposed punishment on humanity for bringing disgrace to the world.

Were the ancient beliefs based on a monotheistic or a polytheistic system? It seems quite clear that African doctrines combined principles of oneness and togetherness, transcendence and immanence, into a unified system; hence they frequently comprised both monotheistic and polytheistic features. Many of the high gods resemble African sacred kings who, like King Kitamba (in *King Kitamba and Queen Muhongo*) reign but do not rule. They occupy the structural centre of the system but are rarely seen or heard and when they are it is only indirectly. Nevertheless, their role is crucial in sustaining the life and progress of the world.

Closer to everyday experience are the lesser divinities and spirits. They usually possess powers that are immanent and they have both a reciprocal and interdependent relationship with mortals. This is clear from the fact that these deities and spirits are perceived through personal encounter as living agents who are directly involved in the lives of the people. Usually they are associated with the elements of nature, such as thunder, lightning (see *Thunder and Lightning*), rain, rivers (see *A House for the Sun and Moon* and *Morning and Evening*), wild animals, forests (see *Chichinguane and Chipfalamfula, Nyambe and Kamunu, Spirits of the Bush, The Sheep God* and *Mokele*). A common form of encounter between the divine and the human is spirit possession and divination: the temporary presence of a deity or spirit in the consciousness of a person. Spirit possession, which is affected by cultural norms and is often highly symbolic, may occur in a formal, ritual context (as in *The Bird Spirit* and *The Spirit of the Rock*) or, as in the case of *The Underwater World*, where the lake god speaks through the diviner in the normal course of everyday life.

Oral Tradition

The tales and narratives in this anthology have, of necessity, been derived from oral tradition: the debris of ancient African mythology where gods, spirits, heroes and heroines, through generations of re-telling, have been dislocated from pre-history and brought forward to later eras. This is a matter of considerable complexity, not one of simple evolution. The poetic and narrative forms of oral transmission among the African peoples living south of the Sahara are remarkably rich and varied and they include not only myths in the traditional sense of symbolic accounts of the origins of phenomena (whether the world, particular cultures, lineages, political structures, or gods), but also songs of praise, epic poetry, folk tales, riddles, proverbs and magic spells. The content of this material also varies considerably and includes children's rhymes and oral history, as well as symbolic texts of profound intellectual significance, such as the highly suggestive tale, *Nyambe and Kamunu*.

Introduction

An important feature of African oral traditions is their close link with music. Poetry exists almost exclusively in chanted form or as song and, among West African peoples with tonal languages (for example, the Akan and the Yoruba), much poetry is recited in musical form rather than spoken or sung.

Myths of Origin

Since many of the African myths that deal with the beginning of the world imply that the origin was an emanation or a growth rather than an act or a specific event, the term 'cosmogony' is more suited to this genre than 'creation myth'. 'Cosmogony' is neutral; 'creation myth' implies a creator and something created and this latter expression is clearly unsuited to a number of the narratives in Chapter 1, Myths of Origin and Extinction. Even the term 'origin' should be used with caution because many of the African myths describing the beginning of things hardly ever have as their focal point the actual origin of the world. The stories rarely are bothered with interpreting or analysing first causes. Instead, cosmogonic myths are concerned with origins only with respect to the foundation or validity of the world as it is. Some of them actually refer to the act of creation as a fashioning of the earth out of raw material that was already present, such as the pre-existing milk in *Doondari and Gueno*, the pre-existing water in *The Formation of Land*, or the pre-existing mud in *Sa and Alatangana*. And in *Fam, the First Man*, the female species has her origins in a magic tree. For the Africans there was never a time when the world was not; there was no beginning in any absolute sense.

Most cosmogonic accounts have certain formal features in common. They refer to irreconcilable opposites, such as heaven and earth (as, for example, in *Nyambe and Kamunu*, *A Home for the*

Sun and Moon, The Bag of Mystic Powers, The Distant Sky, Thunder and Lightning and A Daughter-in-law for Kimanaweze) or darkness and light (as, for example, in Mokele and Sa and Alatangana). In other words, the basic elements of humanity's world and orientation belong to sacred, as opposed to chronological, time: elements both anticipated yet, at the same time, already present, fully realized, constituted, or brought about anew in the narration. Here the accounts transcend the limits of ordinary perception and reason.

The origin of man is usually linked immediately to the cosmogony. Human beings, for instance, may be placed on the earth by a Creator God, or in some other way their origin is from heaven or even from the sea. (For an example of the latter, see Father Moon.) In all cases, however, humans hold a particular place because of their duties to the deity or deities, because of their limitations – or even because of their gifts (see, for example, Fam, the First Man).

In most cosmogonic traditions the final or culminating act is the creation of humanity. The condition of the cosmos prior to the arrival of humans is viewed as separate and distinct from the cultural consequences that result from the presence of men and women on earth. Creation is thus seen as a process of periods or stages, frequently following a trilogy of events. The first stage in the trilogy consists of the world of gods or primordial beings; the second stage is the world of nature (including all non-human living species) and the elements; and the third stage is the world of humans. This tripartite structure is quite evident in Fam, the First Man, The Sheep God and The Formation of Land.

One class of African myth that deals with the advent of humanity on earth also combines this with the beginning of social and religious institutions. These myths clarify both the formation of the cosmos and the social and ethical qualities of human existence. Many African myths of origin speak of a primeval condition of cosmic order and unity and they describe a severance or parting that developed between divinity and humanity, sky and earth, order and disorder, which resulted in conflict. These myths explain why human beings are mortal by telling how they become mortal, thereby assuming that humanity was originally immortal (See *Fam, the First Man*). Occasionally the accounts declare that mortality is the result of an intentional or unintentional misdeed committed by a human being, frequently a woman (as in *The Bag of Mystic Powers*, *Father Moon* and *The Discovery of Fire*) or an animal (as in *The Dog and the Toad* and *The Chameleon and the Lizard*). Although questions of human responsibility are occasionally invoked, the principal meaning is generally that death was a necessary or inevitable outcome, otherwise human beings would not be truly human and humanity and divinity would not be properly separated.

The African tales of origin which offer answers given by humanity to the problems and mysteries of life and death, are rich, exciting and imaginative. In addition to the aforementioned narratives, there is the Kono myth (Guinea) in which Sa, the Bringer of Death, is a primordial power that existed before the Creator God, Alatangana. Again there is the Malozi story from Zambia in which the god Nyambe retreats helplessly from the cruelty of man (see *Nyambe and Kamunu*). In Nigeria, among the Ibo peoples, individuals are permitted by the goddess, Woyengi, to decide on their own fate before entering the world (*The Bag of Mystic Powers*), while the Wapangwa of Tanzania record an extraordinary vision of the earth as having been created from the excrement of ants (*The Sheep God*). The Yoruba of Nigeria regard Obatala, the creator god, as guilty and responsible for deformities in humans because he got drunk on palm wine and thus were born the paraplegics and albinos (see *The Origins of Man*). They also explain the existence of many gods, defining them as all forming part of the one divine being (see *Fam, the First Man*). The most detailed cosmology known, requiring an entire week for its recitation, is that of the Dogon of Mali. And an uncommon and engaging creation tale comes from the Fulani of Mali, a pastoral, cattle-herding tribe whose mythology centres on milk (see *Doondari and Gueno*). The ideas expressed in all of these stories throw light on humanity's relationship to God. They also identify the attempts of men and women to come to terms with the supernatural and the inevitable.

The Yoruba believe that water existed before land (*Fam, the First Man*). The Fang accept an original creation that was condemned and destroyed – not with water but by fire. They also believe in a being that is fallen from grace and sets itself up as the opponent of God (ibid). Numerous African myths develop the notion that humans were originally living in closer harmony with God, as seen in a Sini story from Nigeria which refers to the sky lying close to the earth (*The Distant Sky*). It continues to say that through peoples' own fault the intimate relationship was destroyed. The Malozi of Zambia have a story reminiscent of the Tower of Babel: humanity attempts to equal the god Nyambe by building a tower high into the sky (see *Nyambe and Kamunu*). A similar Yoruba story related the scattering of tribes and languages (*How Humans Were Scattered*). The theme of the forbidden fruit appears among the Efe, and several groups describe the creator god moulding humanity from clay (*The Origin of Man* and *The Bag of Mystic Powers*). The Obatala myth of the Yoruba clearly contains the idea of redemption through suffering (*Obatala and Shango*) and the Wapangwa of Tanzania declare that the Word was the primary force of new creation (*The Sheep God*).

According to nearly all African mythologies, the creator God first agreed to grant humanity immortality, but his message to the world was distorted either through the stupidity or the evil intent of the envoy. Several hundred African variants of the myth of the garbled or perverted message are known (see, for example, *The Dog and the Toad* and *The Chameleon and the Lizard*).

Introduction

Trickster Myths

The best-known type of African folk story is the animal-trickster tale. This category includes satirical stories, characterizations and accounts of the origin of the world. The trickster is a metaphor of life's problems and ambiguities – sometimes the deceiver, but often deceived; sometimes cunning, but often ridiculous; sometimes creative, but often destructive; sometimes wise, but often confused. Order and disorder mark the trickster's actions which may be comic, tragic, or a combination of both. In an attempt to balance opposites, the trickster's negative impulses are actually geared to preparing a new and positive condition and order. Ultimately death gives way to birth, as in the story of *The Two Brothers* where life in the underworld is shown to be more preferable to a mundane existence on earth.

In Bantu Africa (East, Central and southern Africa) and the western Sudan, the trickster is the hare; in West Africa (Ghana, Liberia, Sierra Leone) it is the spider; and in Benin, Nigeria the trickster is the tortoise. The Yoruba consciously poke fun at their own faults when they tell stories of the tortoise-trickster. There are several Tortoise stories in this collection in the Fables chapter. Sometimes the tortoise's cunning defeats itself, as for example, in the tale of the tortoise that steals a calabash from the gods that contains all the wisdom in the world. He hangs it around his neck and is so eager to get home with it that, when he comes to a fallen tree trunk lying across the road, he is unable to get over it because the calabash gets in the way. In his frustration it does not occur to him to put the calabash on his back and in his fury the tortoise smashes it to the ground. Because of this, ever since then, wisdom has been scattered all over the earth in tiny bits and pieces. Anansi, the spider-trickster known to the Akan, often appears as a mythological figure. Sometimes he steals the sky god's stories; sometimes he tricks the god in allowing disease to enter the world. In this capacity he bears some similarity with the Yoruba trickster god, Eshu, who consistently opposes the other gods and thwarts their intentions.

A variant of the trickster tale is the escape story. In it, the hero disentangles himself from an impossible situation by imposing a formidable condition. One such story tells how a cruel chief of Benin ordered his subjects on pain of death to build a new palace but to start at the top and build downward. All were in despair until one wise old man went to the chief and said that they were now ready to begin and could he, as was the tradition, lay the foundation stone.

Dilemma Tales

Stories of another kind, told for entertainment, usually on moonlit nights, are dilemma tales in which the listener is expected to provide the ending or solution. The following is an example of a dilemma tale that circulates among the Wolof of Senegal and Gambia: Three brothers travel to a distant land where they all marry the same girl with whom each sleeps in turn. One night she is murdered by a robber and the eldest brother, with whom she was sleeping, is condemned to death on suspicion. He begs leave to go home and see his father for the last time before he dies. When he is late in returning, the second brother offers to die in his stead. But just as the second brother is about to be executed, the youngest brother comes forward and declares that it was in fact he who had committed the murder. Consequently, the second brother is released and the third takes his place. But just as the third brother is about to be executed, the eldest brother rides in ready to undergo his sentence. Which of the brothers (the audience is asked) is the most noble?

Proverbs and Riddles

According to an Igbo saying, 'Proverbs are the palm oil with which words are eaten'. To a large degree, the art of good conversation and argument depends on their use. By them the speaker does not only demonstrate his erudition but he also is able to attack an antagonist indirectly, without mentioning his name or the subject of the dispute. Some proverbs articulate a community's inherited wisdom and code of behaviour ('If a child washes his hands he will eat with kings' [Igbo]); others identify imagination and a sense of humour ('If the earthworm does not dance in front of the cock, he will still be eaten, but at least the cock cannot say that he was provoked' [Yoruba]).

Riddles usually take the form of a statement, not a question. In the riddle-statement, 'People run away from her when she is pregnant, but they are happy and rejoice when she has delivered', the expected question-ending 'What is she?' is understood, but never actually asked. (The answer is 'a gun'.) Frequently, the riddle is an exercise in metaphorical or allegorical speech, intended to display the questioner's imagination rather than to test the cleverness of the audience. For example, the answer to the Yoruba riddle-statement 'We tie a horse in the house, but its mane flies above the roof,' is 'fire and smoke'.

Myths of Destruction

Myths of eschatology or 'the end' refer not only to death and human mortality but also, in a wider sense, to the destruction of the world. Narratives about the origin of death, for which an added explanation has to be found in the sense that death is not seen as automatically the end of life, are probably as widely diffused as creation stories. One of the most frequently-encountered of such myths tells of a primordial time in which death had no existence as such and explains that it came about as the result of an error, or as a punishment.

One example of a myth about the origin of death may be regarded as characteristic. It appears in various forms in many parts of the sub-Saharan African continent. Among the Zulus the story is told that the creator god, Unkulunkulu, instructed the chameleon to take a message to mankind, saying that all men and women would be granted immortality. But the chameleon, not being in a great hurry, moved very slowly and either stopped to have a meal or fell asleep basking in the sun. In due course the great creator god changed his mind and sent a lizard with just the opposite message to mankind, this time telling them that all people would in fact die. The lizard overtook the chameleon and delivered his message. When the chameleon eventually arrived, his message conflicted with what mankind had already been told by the lizard; no one believed the chameleon and humans were mortal from then on. The Bantu-speaking tribes have a variant with a message that failed and uses the same two characters. Other versions say that the envoy garbled his message and thereby became responsible for humanity's mortality, or that the envoy is purely malicious and deliberately gives a wrong message (as in *The Dog and the Toad*). For the Margi recension, see *The Chameleon and the*

Lizard. In all instances the essence of the myth is that the natural slowness and quickness of the two animal protagonists determine the outcome, making death a natural and inevitable result.

Hero Myths

A significant number of traditions have myths about a culture hero who normally introduces new techniques or technology to benefit humanity, such as the hunter who not only discovered fire, but learned how to use it in cooking food, forging tools and baking pots (see *The Discovery of Fire*). Such heroes may not themselves be responsible for the creation but are the ones who complete the world and make it more habitable for men and women; in other words, they create culture. Ritual institutions, such as marriage, village organization, kingship and priesthood are also important cultural discoveries that have transformed the world for the good of humanity and often the most important deeds of the hero are re-enacted in ritual worship. In some cases, the hero may continue to live among the people in a spiritual form through a high priest or diviner and make an appearance on important cultic occasions. Many African deities are said to have been heroes who died and returned in spiritual form to serve as guardians and protectors of the people. In Africa there is an overlap between myth and history, fact and fiction; together they constitute a unified explanation of the world since the beginning of time.

Conclusion

African myths are not merely light-hearted stories for children, nor are they simply pre-scientific explanations of the cosmos. They are insights, related through narrative, poetry and ceremonial language into a reality that represents the experiences of unique and varied modes of existence. Moreover, these myths express ancient beliefs that have underpinned behavioural patterns, justified social institutions and established customs and values. Consequently, it is scarcely possible to understand the diverse African cultures without an understanding of the mythological traditions. No society can properly be understood in isolation from its myths and certainly this is one good reason for taking them seriously. Frequently, the light which myths cast on the mind of one culture can reveal something about the perceptions and behavioural patterns of another. At a very fundamental level, mythology is a mental process common to all human beings, therefore its articulation in any tradition will, to some degree, be a reflection of ourselves.

1
Myths of Origin and Extinction

Doondari and Gueno

A Fulani Story (Mali)

Before all other things; before time and space; only one object existed: an enormous drop of the whitest milk. Then Doondari descended carrying with him the grey stone. And the stone begat iron; and the iron begat fire; and the fire water; and the water air.

Doondari appeared again in all his glory. He carried with him the grey stone, the cold iron, the hot fire, the cool water. Kneading one into the other he moulded the first Man. The Man had a reasoning brain; he could understand. He knew that he was made from the five elements of life. He became self-satisfied and haughty and, what is more, he even sought to defy Doondari.

So Doondari thought how he could subdue the Man that he had created. To combat Man, Doondari brought in Blindness, and Blindness subdued Man. But Blindness, too, could understand. It knew that it was more powerful than Man; and it in turn grew self-satisfied and haughty.

So Doondari thought how he could subdue the Blindness that he had created. To combat Blindness, Doondari brought in Slumber, and Slumber subdued Blindness. But Slumber, too, could understand many things. It knew, for example, that it was more powerful than Man and Blindness.

So Doondari thought how he could subdue the Slumber that he had created. To combat Slumber, Doondari brought in Anxiety, and Anxiety subdued Slumber. But Anxiety also could understand; for it knew that it was more powerful than Man, Blindness and Slumber. So it in turn grew self-satisfied and haughty.

So Doondari thought how he could subdue the Anxiety that he had created. To combat Anxiety, Doondari brought in his final weapon: Death; and Death subdued Anxiety. But Death, too, could understand. It knew that it was more powerful than Man, Blindness, Slumber and Anxiety. Perhaps he could subdue Doondari himself! In turn, Death grew self-satisfied and haughty.

Once more Doondari appeared, a third time did he descend. But this time he came as Gueno, the eternal and supreme god. And Gueno overcame Death.

Sa and Alatangana

A Kono story (Guinea)

Before the world began there was void and darkness. Nothing existed except for Sa, the Bringer of Death, with his wife and only daughter.

Where was Sa to house his family? With his magic, Sa produced an enormous expanse of grey, slimy mud. No other life or matter did Sa create; only this mass of bubbling mud.

Not long after, the god Alatangana passed that way and wished to pay Sa and his family a visit. But Alatangana was horrified by the dirt and filth of Sa's dwelling. Dismayed and repulsed, the god became extremely angry. He shouted and condemned Sa using the strongest possible language.

'What kind of habitation is this? Who can remain in such an inhospitable place where there is nothing that can live – no vegetation, no living creatures, no light, no beauty!' Thereupon Alatangana banished Sa, his wife and his only daughter from their muddy abode and set out to rectify the situation.

To begin with he gathered the sprawling mud into one area and made it firm and hard. In this way the earth was created. But it was nothing like the earth we know today. There were no trees, no flowers, no rivers, no animals; just dry, solid matter – barren and immensely forlorn.

So Alatangana set about to diversify the landscape with areas of water in which swam all kinds of fish. On the land he raised mountains and dug valleys, produced greenery and all kinds of animal life. In the skies, multi-coloured birds flew in enormous flocks. The earth was totally alive, active, and it laughed with delight.

Sa was immensely pleased with these improvements to his former, dirty abode. Out of gratitude, he offered generous hospitality to Alatangana and thanked him deeply for his industry and concern. After this they became close friends and the god was a constant visitor at Sa's home.

Time passed, and Alatangana fell in love with Sa's only daughter. He was, after all, unmarried and life was often very lonely. Eventually, he summoned up enough courage to ask his friend for his blessing to wed the young lady. Sa, however, was extremely attached to his daughter and could not bear the thought of parting with her, in spite of his indebtedness to Alatangana. Again and again Sa invented excuses and postponed giving an answer. Finally he had to refuse openly the god's request.

But Alatangana realized soon enough what was afoot. He could see what was going on in Sa's mind. So the god devised a plan and made a secret negotiation with his beloved. One night, when dark clouds covered the skies, they eloped and married. And in order to escape the certain wrath of Sa, they went to live in a very distant land.

Their life together was happy and prosperous and they had a very large family – fourteen children in all: four white and three black boys; four white and three black girls. What surprised the parents more than their skin colour was the fact that these children spoke in an amazing assortment of strange languages which Alatangana and his wife could not understand. Bewildered by this, and summoning up considerable courage, the god set out to make his peace with Sa, his father-in-law, and to ask him about this extraordinary phenomenon. Sa received his son-in-law with considerable indignation.

'This was sent to punish you, Alatangana, for what you did to me. By my magic I have given strange tongues to my grandchildren. You and your wife will never understand what your children are saying. However, if you wish to be reconciled to me, you must have the white children wed among themselves, and the black children to do the same. In this way, the earth will be peopled by many white and black tribes. If you do this I shall ease your pain and give the gifts of reason and script to your white children so that they may communicate their thoughts in writing. But to your black children I shall grant the ability to till and to cultivate the land so that they may never grow hungry. They shall wield the pick, the hoe, and the axe.

'I also charge you, Alatangana,' added Sa, 'to forbid your white children from marrying the black, and to forbid the black children from marrying the white. Let the white only marry the white, and the black, black.'

Anxious to become reconciled to his father-in-law, Alatangana agreed to every word and when he returned to his distant home and to his family, he immediately arranged for the seven marriages: four white grooms with their four white brides, and three black grooms with their three black brides. After the celebrations the newly-weds set out to all parts of the world and produced all the races of mankind. They were humanity's first ancestors.

Myths of Origin and Extinction

But the offspring of Alatangana's children were still left to dwell in darkness, for light had not yet shone on their lands. So once again Alatangana had to speak to his father-in-law, Sa. But instead of going himself, he sent two ambassadors, the red tou-tou and the golden cock: the two earliest risers of all the birds.

'Alatangana has sent us to you, great Sa. He asks that you shed light on the lands of his children and grandchildren so that they may work for a living and enjoy the creation. We have travelled far, O great one, for see how Alatangana has provided us with food and money for our journey.'

Sa listened to the message of the two birds, the red tou-tou and the golden cock, and took pity on them.

'Come in, come in,' he said warmly. 'Let me tell you a great secret. There is indeed light for the world but it can only be summoned through musical sounds. Sit down and I shall teach you the song of light. With its tones you will shed radiant beams over Alatangana's children and grandchildren and they will be able to work for a living and enjoy the creation.'

When the red tou-tou and the golden cock returned to Alatangana with Sa's response, the god became furious. 'I sent you on an important mission, I gave you money and food for the journey, and all you have to offer me is a song? Prepare to die!'

But just as Alatangana was about to strike them down, the red tou-tou let out its plaintive cry and the golden cock also lifted up its voice to the heavens and filled the air with song. In an instant the first light of the first day enveloped them. It was a miracle! Alatangana regretted his words and asked the birds to forgive him; whereupon the sun rose above the horizon and began its royal journey across the sky, following the route established by Sa. At the end of the day, the sun settled and rested at a place on the opposite side of the earth.

But light did not disappear altogether for the night sky was filled with the stars, the planets and the moon. These, too, shed their light on the world for the benefit of man during the darkness of night. From that time onwards, the two birds must sing their song in order to summon light. First the little red tou-tou and after it the golden cock.

Sa said to himself, 'Look at what I have done for that scoundrel Alatangana: what now must he do for me?'

So Sa summoned the god and said to him: 'I have given you the sun, the moon, the planets and the stars so that your children and grandchildren may work for their living and enjoy the creation. But what have you done for me? You snatched away my only child and took her to the end of the earth. Have you no better service to render me? For depriving me of my child, you must in turn present me with one of yours at any time that I care to bid for one. When the child hears the rattle of a calabash in his dreams, he or she will know that Sa has called. This sound shall be my voice and it must never be disobeyed.'

Alatangana knew that he was guilty of a great misdeed. He had no choice but to consent. Thus it is that because Alatangana neglected the tradition of paying the bride-price that humanity is subject to death and annihilation.

How Humans Were Scattered

The ancient and sacred city of Ife lies at the heart of the Yoruba culture. It is believed by the Yoruba to have been the place of creation and the centre of the world. This Yoruba story explains how humans became scattered into different tribes with different languages.

Once, long ago, all people lived in one town, called Ife, and they all spoke one simple language, Yoruba. In those days everyone was equal in all respects. Their skin was the same colour, they were all good at the same things, they were all equally strong, equally beautiful, and equally healthy. Everyone had enough of what they needed, but no one had too much. If anyone needed something, they had only to inform God's messenger, and he would tell God, who would provide them with what they needed. So there were always enough yams, corn, fruit and millet and the other basic necessities of life.

There was only one problem. People were bored. They had everything they needed, and everyone was the same, so they found life dull. One day someone spoke up.

'All of us in Ife are the same. We all have the same colour skin. We all look the same. None of us owns more than anyone else. We all like the same things. We all speak the same way in the same language. How boring! Wouldn't it be nice if we were all different and did different things?'

Everyone agreed. They wanted a change. So they started complaining to God's messenger, asking for different things. Some wanted a bigger house. Some wanted different colour skin. Some wanted to speak differently. Some wanted to be more clever. Some wanted extra yams and some wanted more land to farm. So it went on. In the beginning the messenger would faithfully carry all their demands to God and God would listen patiently. But after a while God became irritated. He told the messenger what to tell them. The messenger went back to the people.

'God says you are to be content with what he has given you. He has deliberately arranged things in this way so that you will not have anything to quarrel with each other about. He wants everything to be fair and no one to be unjustly deprived and no one to have more than their share. This is how he wants it to be.' But the people were not happy.

'Tell God he must give us what we ask, or we will revolt against him. We will have nothing more to do with him. We will organize our affairs the way we want them, without his help.'

The messenger went back to God and reported what they had said.

'Very well,' said God, 'let them have what they want.'

So everything began to change. The one who wanted brown skin got it, and the one who wanted light-coloured skin got it. Those who wanted money got it, others got more land. Some received servants and slaves, some more yams. Soon they began to quarrel. Some felt that they had not been given enough of what they wanted, and that others had been given too much. They started feeling suspicious of people whose colour was different from their own, or who spoke differently from them. They began to talk in different languages. Previously they had all spoken one language but now they found themselves speaking Swahili, Ibo, Hausa or Arabic, and one could not understand another. Fights broke out and people became afraid. So they began to migrate in different directions to find safety. Some went north, some east, some south and some west. They settled in different places and developed different customs and religions. Thus the different tribes of the world came into being.

Once, in the beginning, everyone was equal. They all lived peacefully in Ife. Then they were scattered and to this day all people suffer from suspicion, envy and the wish to have more than others.

King Kitamba and Queen Muhongo

A Bantu myth (the Ambundu of Angola)

The principal wife of Kitamba, a chieftain who ruled in the village of Kasanji, died very suddenly. Her name was Queen Muhongo and the bereaved Kitamba mourned her for many days. Not only did he mourn himself, but he ordered that all of his subjects mourn as well, as a sign of their common grief.

'In Kasanji,' declared the chieftain, 'no man shall do any work. The youngsters may not play and shout; the women may neither pound nor knead; no one in the village shall speak.'

His fifteen counsellors complained bitterly about this ruling, but Kitamba remained firm, and proclaimed that he would not eat or speak nor would he allow anyone else to do either until his beloved queen was restored to him.

The counsellors called a meeting one morning and summoned a witch doctor who, having first received his fee (a weapon and a cow) and hearing their side of the story, announced, 'Leave everything to me.' He then set off to gather some herbs which he pounded in a medicine mortar. To this mixture he added some water and after this commanded that the chieftain and all the people of Kasanji wash themselves with it.

'Send me some men to dig a grave in my guest hut at the hearth,' directed the witch doctor. Four able-bodied workers were immediately despatched to do the job, and at its completion the witch doctor entered the grave with his own young son, saying the following words to his wife: 'Remove your brightly coloured garments and put on your clothes of mourning. Every day you must pour water on the hearth.' Then the men filled in the grave with earth.

Ahead of him the witch doctor saw a road open up so he and his young son walked along it until he came to a village, and there he saw Queen Muhongo seated and sewing a basket. When she saw them approaching, the queen raised her head and asked, 'Where have you come from and why are you here?'

'It is you that I seek,' replied the witch doctor. 'For since your death your husband, King Kitamba, will neither eat nor drink nor speak. In your home village the men do not work, the youngsters do not shout and play, the women do not pound or knead. No one is allowed to speak, for all must mourn the loss of the queen. King Kitamba has declared that only when his beloved Muhongo is restored to him will he talk, eat and drink. It is for this reason that I have come to you.'

Queen Muhongo then pointed out a man seated a little way off. 'Do you know who that man is?' she inquired of the witch doctor.

'I have no idea,' he replied.

'That is Lord Kalunga and all he does is devour us, all of us.'

Directing his attention to another man, this time one who was chained to a rock, the queen asked the witch doctor whether or not he knew him. And he answered: 'Strangely enough he strongly resembles King Kitamba, whom I left from whence I have come.'

'You have answered correctly,' answered Queen Muhongo.

Yes, it was indeed Kitamba and the appearance of his wraith in the underworld was a sign that he had not many years to live. Queen Muhongo continued: 'Here in Kalunga's realm one never arrives in order to return. But let me give you the bone bracelet that was buried with me. You can show it to my husband Kitamba as a proof that you have really visited the land of the dead. But you must promise me that you will never mention to the king that you saw him in this place. One more thing, you yourselves must eat nothing in this underworld otherwise you will never be allowed to return to earth.'

Meanwhile, the witch doctor's wife had kept pouring water on the grave by the hearth. One day she saw the earth beginning to crack and break; the cracks opened wider and finally her husband's head issued forth. He gradually made his way out, and pulled his small son up after him. The little boy fainted when he came out into the sunlight, so his father washed him with some herbal medicine which soon revived him.

On the following day the witch doctor went to the counsellors and described all that he had seen and heard. Of course he refused to reveal his sighting of King Kitamba in the underworld. When he received a further payment of two slaves, the witch doctor returned to his home.

The counsellors made their report to King Kitamba and showed him the bone bracelet. 'In truth this is the very same one,' commented the king, and with this he countermanded the official mourning. The men resumed their work, the young boys and girls their playing and shouting, the women their pounding and kneading, and everyone ate and drank in abundance. Then, after a few years King Kitamba died and joined his beloved queen in the realm of Lord Kalunga. The people of Kasanji wailed at his funeral and bestowed him with many honours.

The Chameleon and the Lizard

A Margi story (Central African Republic)

When Death made his first appearance in the world, the people were completely taken aback. So they chose the chameleon as their representative and sent him with a message to the high god. They wanted to know why the god had sent Death to them.

The god spoke these words to the chameleon. 'Tell the humans that if they want the dead to revive they must throw boiled grain over the corpse.'

Now the chameleon took a long time to return to the people with the god's reply and in the meantime Death raged throughout their households. Many people lost their lives. In despair, the survivors chose another envoy, the lizard, to ask the same question of the high god.

The lizard reached the kingdom of the high god a short time after the chameleon had said what he had to say. But the high god was very annoyed at being asked the same question twice. So he said, 'Tell the humans that they should dig a hole in the ground and bury their dead in it.'

On his return the lizard overtook the chameleon and delivered his message first, so that when the chameleon finally arrived the dead were already buried in the ground.

Therefore, because of humanity's impatience, men and women were deprived of immortality.

The Dog and the Toad

An Ibo story (Nigeria)

When Death made his first appearance in the world, the people chose a dog to act as their representative. The dog was sent with a message to the god Chuku, 'Is it possible for the dead to be restored to life again and to be sent back to their homes and families?' But instead of going straight to Chuku with the message, the dog delayed.

The toad, however, had overheard the message, and because he wanted to get his revenge on mankind for past problems, he sped ahead of the dog and got to Chuku first.

'I have been sent by the humans to tell you their wish,' said the deceitful toad. 'They say that after they die they have no desire whatsoever to return to their homes and families in the world.'

'Tell them their wish is granted,' said Chuku. In a little while the dog approached Chuku with the original message, but Chuku was unable to change his decision.

Therefore, while it is true that a human can be born again, he or she will never return with the same body or the same characteristics.

The Bag of Mystic Powers

An Ijo story (Nigeria)

At the beginning of time there existed an enormous field, and in this field stood a gigantic Iroko tree with large supporting trunks. At the end of the field appeared pairs of men and women. Each woman held a broom and each man carried a bag. The women began sweeping the field while their partners collected the dirt into their bags. And the dirt transformed into charms of which some collected ten or more, while others none at all. When the area was swept clean, the workers disappeared back into the sides of the field, two by two.

Shortly the sky grew dark and from the clouds there was lowered onto the field a large table, a correspondingly large chair, and a huge Creation Stone. On the table was a big mound of earth. The thunder boomed, lightning flashed and Woyengi (the Mother) appeared from on high. At once she sat on the large chair and placed her feet on the Creation Stone. Using the earth that was on the huge table, Woyengi formed human beings. At first they were lifeless and without gender. So Woyengi embraced each one and breathed the breath of life into them so that they became living, rational creatures. But they were still neither male nor female. One by one Woyengi asked them, 'Choose for yourself which you would prefer to be: man or woman.'

Then Woyengi asked each and every one about how they would like to live their life on earth. The responses varied. One sought wealth, another many children, another a short or long life, and all manner of things. To each, according to his or her wish, Woyengi granted the gift. Finally Woyengi asked them how they would like to die in order to return to her. And each one selected a disease from among the numerous afflictions that were known on earth. To all of these wishes, Woyengi said, 'So be it.'

Among this group of newly-created humanity were two who asked to be women. One asked Woyengi that her children become rich and famous while the other, named Ogboinba, only desired special powers, mystic powers, that no other person in the world would possess. Both of these women asked to be born in the same city.

Eventually Woyengi took these new human creatures, both men and women, to two streams. These streams, which led to the dwelling place of mankind, were of two sorts – one was muddy and the other was clear. Into the muddy stream Woyengi conducted all those who had asked her for wealth, material possessions and many children, while into the clear stream went all those whose requests were not for worldly things.

Thus did Ogboinba and the other woman come to be born in the same city and ended up becoming the closest of companions. Together as youngsters they played games, ate, shared secrets, and slept in the same room. It was as if they were siblings, being born of the same parents. But Ogboinba clearly displayed some extraordinary gifts. Even from an early age she had the power to heal and to cure and it was also evident that she was a clairvoyant. Moreover, she possessed the ability to understand the languages of birds and animals, of trees, and even of the grass and rushes. Her prophesies always transpired into realities and she could perform strange and wonderful acts. Inevitably, everyone spoke about her.

In later life both Ogboinba and her dear friend became brides to men of that same city and before long Ogboinba's friend had her first child. But Ogboinba had no baby and was not even expecting one. In the meantime, her magic powers continued to increase. Again her friend became a mother to another infant, but still nothing for Ogboinba. Nevertheless, her reputation spread to all quarters and she became the most sought-after healer of all time. But in spite of her extraordinary fame, Ogboinba was distressed. Her life was empty without children; she wanted one badly. She fretted and yearned to be a mother.

Her friend continued to bear more and more babies, for this in fact was what she had requested from Woyengi, and Ogboinba loved each and every one of them. She took care of them using her mystic gifts just as if they were her own offspring. But still she was not satisfied. What she really desired with all her heart was children of her own to raise and love. According to what she had asked of Woyengi, her supernatural powers continued to increase. But there was no joy in the depths of her being.

Finally Ogboinba found the entire situation unbearable so she thought up a plan. She decided to make a secret trip back to

Woyengi in order to be recreated, this time as a mother of children. One day, therefore, she entered her special medicine room – this is where she stored her magic powers – and asked them one by one if they would come with her on her mission to Woyengi. None of the potions or medicines refused, but Ogboinba would not take them all. Consequently, into a bag she placed only the most potent remedies and cures and the most mystic powers. Then she visited her friend with all the children and said, 'I bid you farewell, for I am about to embark upon a special journey.' Her friend was very sad indeed for they had never parted company since childhood, not even for a day. It would be so unnatural not seeing Ogboinba for any length of time; and what is more, her children would be deprived of the special protection that they had been enjoying for so long.

'Do not fear,' replied Ogboinba. 'I promise you that even in my absence the children will still be under my protection. No harm will come to them.' At this, Ogboinba took her leave and set off on her journey to find Woyengi.

The road leading out of the city was wide and dusty. Ogboinba trudged along it with her bag of special powers and remedies slung over her shoulder. This wide road stopped by the edge of a large mangrove forest, and beyond the forest was the open sea. In the mangrove forest lived Isembi, the king. Ogboinba walked steadily day and night, neither eating nor sleeping. In the distance she could hear the sound of the sea, its waves crashing against the rocky shore. As she approached, the sound increased in volume. But before reaching the sea, Ogboinba reached the kingdom of Isembi: the mangrove forest.

Unafraid, our traveller picked her way through the trees and after a few moments she heard a voice. Ogboinba stopped dead in her tracks. The voice called out from behind her. When she turned around Ogboinba saw Isembi himself. To her utter surprise, the king knew her name: 'You must be the famous Ogboinba that everyone talks about. Is that not so?' asked Isembi indignantly.

'In the entire world there is only one Ogboinba,' replied our heroine fearlessly, 'and I am she.'

'Well, I must say, you have few manners,' snapped Isembi icily, 'for you did not have the courtesy to call on me as king of this mangrove forest. Everyone here knows about your extraordinary skills. We are in fact most honoured to have you among us like this. Do come to my palace.'

Ogboinba was hardly in a position to refuse, so she went with King Isembi to his palace and was wined and dined in a most sumptuous manner. After enjoying the hospitality Ogboinba insisted that she ought to be on her way. 'What is your destination?' asked the king.

'I am bound for Woyengi,' said Ogboinba. 'For many years now I have been married but have been unable to bear a child. So I am going to Woyengi with the request that she recreate me.'

'But this is out of the question,' cried Isembi. 'You must not even attempt such a thing. Do you not know that it is impossible to see Woyengi while you are still alive? This mission will end in disaster – turn back, turn back!'

'My mind is completely made up,' replied Ogboinba. 'Even though I am still alive, I must see Woyengi.'

Thereupon she took her leave of Isembi, slung the bag of powers over her shoulder, departed from the mangrove kingdom, and headed toward the sea. After she had gone but a short distance, Ogboinba stopped in her tracks, thought deeply, and turned back to Isembi.

'I would like you to test your powers against mine. Consider this a challenge!' declared Ogboinba.

'I will not engage in battle with a woman. How dare you insult me,' replied Isembi. 'Depart from here this instant.'

'I insist that we have a trial of powers. A woman I may be, but I challenge you nonetheless, and you must accept,' cried Ogboinba.

Enraged now, and choking with anger, Isembi turned to the fearless woman and poured scorn upon her: 'Have you not been informed of my powers? I am Isembi the invincible, king of the forest. Do you dare challenge me like this – you, a mere woman! Prepare, now, to meet your end!'

At this, Isembi went into his medicine hut and consulted his powers and potions. All of them displayed signs of resistance. But the king was not to be disgraced by such things, especially at this time when there was a female opponent. Thus, in spite of the warnings, he went back to Ogboinba with as many magic potions and powers that he felt to be necessary. It was time to destroy this arrogant woman.

King Isembi chose a large clearing in the forest for the contest and asked Ogboinba to apply her mystic powers on him first. Ogboinba flatly refused. 'You, O great king, are older and wiser. It is only fitting that you subject me to your mystic powers.' Anxious to do away with her without further delay, Isembi performed his magic incantations over and over again. All at once the many remedies and powers in Ogboinba's bag disappeared. The bag was completely empty!

Now it was Ogboinba's turn. She lifted up her voice, cried out her own incantations, and danced a stately circle dance around Isembi in order to obliterate his powers. While she did this, her own mystic powers and remedies returned to her bag, one by one. By the time she had finished her chant and dance, all of her magic had returned to the bag. She was her old self once more.

'O King Isembi,' she cried, 'try your powers on me once more, but this time use all that you have, omitting none.'

'I have none more powerful than the ones already used, O warrior woman. Now you must subject me to your powers – that is, if you have any.'

Ogboinba began her incantations again, uttering her chant and dancing in a circle around her opponent. As she did these things, all of Isembi's powers and potions disappeared from his bag and entered hers. Isembi himself fell down dead.

Then she slung her bag over her shoulder and set off again on her journey. She had not proceeded more than a few steps when Isembi's queen called out imploringly, 'Come back, come back,

Ogboinba. Bring my husband back to life, I beg of you.' Ogboinba herself had a husband and was moved by the plaint of the queen. So she returned to the clearing and after intoning some of her incantations, Isembi was revived. But the queen begged for something more: she asked Ogboinba to return her husband's powers and potions. 'His life I returned to you, O queen,' replied Ogboinba, 'but Isembi's powers are now my powers.' And with this she left to continue her journey.

Shortly thereafter, Ogboinba left the mangrove forest far behind her and reached the city of King Egbe by the seashore. As she walked through it, she heard a voice call out to her from behind. Turning around, she saw that it was the king himself.

'Are you not the Ogboinba that everyone talks so much about?' asked the king.

'In the entire world there is only one Ogboinba,' she replied fearlessly, 'and I am she.'

'Well, I must say, you have few manners,' snapped Egbe coldly, 'for you did not have the courtesy to call upon me as king of this city by the sea. Everyone here knows your extraordinary skills. We are, in fact, most honoured to have you among us like this. Do come to my palace.'

Ogboinba was hardly in a position to refuse; so she went with King Egbe to his palace and was wined and dined in a most sumptuous manner. After enjoying the hospitality, Ogboinba insisted that she really ought to be on her way.

'What is your destination?' asked the king.

'I am bound for Woyengi,' replied Ogboinba. 'For many years now I have been married but have been unable to bear a child. So I am going to Woyengi with the request that she recreate me.'

'But this is out of the question,' cried Egbe. 'You must not even attempt such a thing. Do you not know that it is impossible to see Woyengi while you are still alive? This mission will end in disaster – turn back, turn back!'

'My mind is completely made up,' replied Ogboinba. 'Even though I am still alive, I must see Woyengi.'

Thereupon she took her leave of Egbe, slung the bag of powers over her shoulder, departed from the kingdom by the sea, and continued her journey. After she had gone but a short distance, Ogboinba stopped in her tracks, thought deeply, and turned back to the king.

'I would like to test your powers against mine, O Egbe. Consider this a challenge!' declared Ogboinba.

'I will not engage in battle with a woman. How dare you insult me,' answered the astonished Egbe. 'Depart from here this instant!'

'I insist that we have a trial of powers. A woman I may be, but I challenge you, and you must accept,' cried Ogboinba.

Enraged now, and choking with anger, Egbe turned to the fearless woman and poured scorn upon her: 'Have you not been told about my prowess? I am Egbe the all-powerful king of the city by the sea. Go on your way; you are a mere woman. Or prepare to meet your end!'

At this Egbe went into his medicine hut and gathered up all of his most potent medicines – the ones that were the most efficacious whenever the king was confronted by challenges of this kind.

'First you must submit me to your magic powers,' declared King Egbe. As usual, Ogboinba flatly refused.

'You, O great king, are older and wiser. It is only fitting that you apply your mystic forces on me first.' Anxious to do away with her without further delay, Egbe sang his magic incantations over and over again. All at once, the many medicines and powers in Ogboinba's bag including those of Isembi that she had secured, were dispersed in many directions. Egbe's magic had emptied the bag completely.

Now it was Ogboinba's turn. She lifted up her voice, cried out her own incantations, and danced a stately circle dance around Egbe in order to obliterate his magic. When she did this, her own mystic powers, as well as those of Isembi, returned to the bag, one by one. By the time that she had finished her chant and her dance, everything had returned to the bag. She was her old self once more.

'O King Egbe,' exclaimed Ogboinba, 'try your powers on me once more, but this time use all that you have, omitting none.'

'But I have none more powerful than the ones I have already used, O warrior woman. Now you must submit me to your powers – that is, if you have any.'

So Ogboinba began her incantations again, uttering her chant and dancing in a circle around her opponent. As she did these things, all of Egbe's powers and potions entered her bag and when she stopped, the king fell down dead. Thus having defeated King Egbe, Ogboinba left to continue her journey to the wide sea with the medicine bag slung over her shoulder. The bag now bulged with the combined magic forces of Ogboinba, Isembi and Egbe and the weight began to weary our heroine.

She had not proceeded more than a few steps when Egbe's queen called out imploringly, 'Come back, come back, Ogboinba. Bring my husband back to life, I beg of you.' Her weeping touched Ogboinba's heart and she took pity on the queen. So she returned and after intoning some of her incantations, Egbe was revived. But the queen begged for something more – she asked Ogboinba to return her husband's mystic powers and potions.

'His life I returned to you, O queen,' replied Ogboinba, 'but Egbe's powers are now my powers.' And with this she departed from the city by the sea to continue her journey.

Finally Ogboinba arrived at the edge of a roaring ocean. This turbulent stretch of water had never been crossed by a living person. Its immense waves crashed like thunder on the rocks and roared through the cliffside caves. The sights and sounds struck terror into the soul of Ogboinba. However, nothing could change her from her resolve or shatter her tenacity. She had to cross the ocean; she could not – she would not – turn back.

While she was staring at the ocean and wondering what to do next, to Ogboinba's astonishment, a deafening voice boomed out from the stormy waters: 'Go no further; I am the mighty Ocean. No one passes over me. Beware!' Mustering up her courage and finding her voice, Ogboinba spoke out: 'In the entire world there is only one Ogboinba and I am she. I seek the great Mother Woyengi; I must cross the ocean.' Again the voice bellowed forth: 'You have been warned, go no further. I am the mighty Ocean; no one passes over me. Beware or I shall swallow you whole!' This message terrified Ogboinba. But her desire for a baby overcame all her fears and she knew that the only way to have her wish granted was for her to see Woyengi. Nothing must stop her, nothing.

With tremendous boldness and great faith Ogboinba walked across the sand and entered the ocean depths. The waves bubbled towards her and covered her feet. The tide kept rising and soon her ankles were under the water, then her knees and her thighs. Fear overcame her; she remained totally rooted in one spot. Ogboinba could move neither backwards nor forwards but remained fixed while the sea climbed higher and higher towards her waist and neck. Her first thoughts went to the precious bag of mystic powers. She lifted it high above her head but still the sea continued to rise, higher and higher, now to her chin.

Finally Ogboinba cried out in trepidation, 'Are you really the Ocean that is impassable? Can this be true?' After which she began her incantations, repeating them over and over again. As she did so, the ocean waters began to fall back and soon they swirled lower and lower, below her chest, her legs, and down to her feet. Eventually the ocean bed itself lay exposed and dry. Ogboinba could even catch sight of the gods and spirits of the sea who were obviously astonished at these happenings.

Therefore Ogboinba, with the bag of mystic powers in her hands, walked dry-shod along the bed of the ocean to the opposite shore. At that point she turned back, ordered the sea to resume its former place, and continued on her journey.

After some time our traveller chanced across another kingdom. This one was ruled by King Tortoise and Queen Opoin. King Tortoise's parents, Alika and Ariya also lived there with their children and grandchildren. Now as Ogboinba was walking along, King Tortoise spotted her and called to her by name.

'Are you not the Ogboinba that I have heard so much about?' he asked. Ogboinba delivered her usual reply: 'In the entire world there is only one Ogboinba, and I am she.'

'Do come to my palace,' said King Tortoise. 'We have known about you for such a long time. It would be an honour for us to get to know you better.' So Ogboinba went with the king to his palace where she was fed a sumptuous meal. After enjoying the hospitality, Ogboinba insisted that she really ought to be on her way.

'How is it that you are on this side of the ocean? Neither man nor woman lives over here. What do you seek?'

'I am bound for Woyengi,' said Ogboinba. 'For many years now I have been married but have been unable to bear a child. So I am going to Mother Woyengi with the request that she recreate me.'

'But this is out of the question,' cried King Tortoise. 'You must not even attempt such a thing. Do you not know that it is impossible to see Woyengi while you are still alive? This mission will end in disaster – turn back, turn back!'

'My mind is completely made up,' replied Ogboinba. 'Even though I am still alive, I must see Woyengi.'

'But I have to warn you,' advised King Tortoise, 'just a little way from here dwell the gods Ada and Yisa. Both are great and powerful deities and the latter possesses two small Creating Stones. No one has ever passed that way. You must complete your journey here.'

'Nothing can stop me now,' insisted Ogboinba. So she took her leave of King Tortoise, slung the heavy bag of mystic powers over her shoulder, departed from Tortoise's kingdom, and continued on her relentless journey. After she had gone but a short distance, Ogboinba stopped in her tracks, thought deeply, and turned back to King Tortoise. She challenged him with her usual request for a trial of powers to which the king replied scornfully: 'Do you not know who I am? I am celebrated in all parts of the world for my mystic powers. Can you, a mere woman, possibly withstand my magic?' At this, Tortoise went into his medicine hut and gathered up all of his most fearful forces and mystic potions.

'Try out your powers on me first,' said Ogboinba.

'Impossible. I am a man and the king of this city. You must begin,' replied Tortoise.

'I insist, O great king. Please begin.' So Tortoise commenced his incantations, chanting them over and over again. All at once Ogboinba's bag dropped to the ground and all the powers and medicines therein scattered to the ends of the earth.

In retaliation, Ogboinba pronounced her own incantations and danced a stately dance around her opponent. Immediately the bag returned to her hand, followed by the mystic powers, one by one. By the time she finished her chant and her dance, everything had returned to the bag. She was her old self once more.

'O King Tortoise,' she cried, 'try out your mystic powers on me once more, but this time use all that you have, omitting none.'

'But I have none more powerful than the ones already used, O warrior woman. Now you must expose me to your powers – that is, if you have any.'

Taking her turn, Ogboinba began her incantations again, rendering with intensity her chant and dancing in a circle around the king. As she did these things, King Tortoise fell down dead while all of his potions and powers entered her swelling bag. With Tortoise thus out of the way, Ogboinba took up her load and left to continue her journey. She had not proceeded more than a few steps when she heard the weeping and wailing of Queen Opoin. Grief-stricken, the queen called out pathetically, 'Come back, come back Ogboinba. Bring my husband back to life, I beg of you.' Her lament touched Ogboinba's heart and she took pity on the queen. So, returning, she raised King Tortoise back to life with her mystic powers and resumed her journey. But before Ogboinba left the city, Queen Opoin begged for something more: she asked Ogboinba to restore her husband's magic forces and mystic potions.

'His life I returned to you, O gracious Queen Opoin,' announced Ogboinba, 'but your husband's forces and potions are now mine.'

Ogboinba walked and walked for several days and nights, the weighty burden once more slung across her shoulder. Eventually she reached the kingdom of the god Ada who, on seeing her, questioned her in the usual way.

'In the entire world there is only one Ogboinba, and I am she,' came the standard response.

'I forbid a person as famous as you to continue your journey without visiting my palace,' insisted Ada.

Ogboinba was hardly in a position to refuse, so she went with Ada to his palace and was wined and dined in a manner befitting the guest of a god and king. After thanking her host for his generous hospitality, Ogboinba declared that she really ought to be on her way.

'But what has brought you here to the abode of the gods? Yours are the first human feet ever to have trodden on this ground. No mortal creature has ever been here before. Why then have you come?' Ogboinba gave her usual reply.

'But this is out of the question,' cried Ada. 'You must not even attempt such a thing. No one ever lays eyes on Woyengi, not even me!'

'My mind is completely made up,' replied Ogboinba, 'for my desire to bear a child is so great and so inexpressible that no obstacle could ever prevent me from seeing the great goddess, no matter where she might be.'

Thereupon she took her leave of the god Ada, slung the bag of mystic powers across her shoulder, and left to continue her journey. After she had gone but a short distance, Ogboinba stopped in her tracks, thought deeply, and turned back to Ada.

'I wish to test your powers against mine. Consider this a challenge!' announced the audacious Ogboinba. Imagine Ada's astonishment at such a request! All he could do was to ask his visitor whether or not she really meant what he imagined he had heard. Our stubborn heroine simply responded by repeating her challenge. Whereupon Ada went into his medicine hut and carefully examined his pots and jars of potions. To his utter disbelief, the contents of each and every one had turned into thick, red blood!

'This could scarcely be a serious warning,' he thought. 'After all, she is only a human being, and a woman at that!'

Therefore, ignoring the sign, Ada armed himself with his medicines and powers and instructed Ogboinba to test him with her mystic forces first. As usual, Ogboinba refused and infuriated the god by insisting that he deal the first blow. Immediately, Ada directed all his magic power on Ogboinba who fell prostrate, as if dead. However, she managed to regain her composure, stood up, and responded to the attack with her own incantations, chant and dance. As she circled around the god, all of Ada's energies left him and entered Ogboinba's bag of mystic powers. Finally, Ada fell down dead. Triumphant once more, Ogboinba raised up her load and continued her journey on the stony and dusty road.

Day after day she walked, night after night. No one could help but admire her perseverance. Finally she reached the kingdom of the greatest and most powerful of the gods, Yasi. Yasi had actually been aware of Ogboinba's movements for some time. He had seen her and followed her progress even when she was very, very far away. Now that she had managed to reach his realm he asked her if she was not the renowned Ogboinba that everyone spoke about. The traveller gave her customary reply: 'In the entire world there is only one Ogboinba, and I am she.'

'I am the king of this territory,' said Yasi. 'Come to my palace and I shall give you some food and drink.' Ogboinba was hardly in a position to refuse, so she went to the god's palace and was wined and dined in a manner befitting the guest of a god and king. After thanking her host for his generous hospitality Ogboinba insisted that she really ought to be on her way.

'Why are you undertaking this long journey?' asked Yasi.

'For many years now I have been married but have been unable to bear a child. So I am going to Mother Woyengi with the request that she recreate me,' replied Ogboinba.

'Do you realize that no living person has ever seen Woyengi? Turn back before it is too late!' But Ogboinba remained stubborn and would not accept the advice.

'I have to continue my journey,' she insisted.

So she lifted up her heavy bag of mystic powers and set out from Yasi's kingdom. As before, she stopped after a short while, thought deeply, came back, and confronted the god with her request for a trial of powers. Yasi was astounded at this audacity.

'Could you repeat what you just said?' he asked. 'I thought I heard you challenge me to compete with you in a trial of powers.'

'That is completely true,' replied Ogboinba brazenly. 'I wish to put your powers to the test.'

Red with anger, Yasi spoke these words: 'Do you not know that I am the greatest and most powerful of all the gods? How dare you, a mere human being – and a woman at that – make such a provocative demand. It would be nothing for me to strike you down. Go your way and be thankful that I have shown you mercy!'

'I insist on testing your mystic powers against mine. Let the contest begin,' declared the warrior woman.

Furious and flustered, Yasi rushed into his medicine hut where he was horrified to discover that the contents of all his pots and jars had turned into thick, red blood.

'Impossible!' he cried. 'How can this be? She is but a weak human creature. I will show her the contest that she wants!' Yasi took up the two small Creating Stones, approached his opponent, and invited her to begin the match. As usual, Ogboinba refused and insisted that Yasi begin. There was no time for dallying, so Yasi hurled the full force of his magic powers onto his opponent. The result was that Ogboinba's head was immediately separated from her body and shot straight up into the clouds. Meanwhile, the rest of her stood fast and her right hand grasped the bag of mystic powers.

Before long Ogboinba's head returned from the clouds and attached itself once more to her body. Ogboinba was, therefore, again totally whole and alive. After this Ogboinba said to Yasi: 'Try again, but this time with all of your mystic powers. Omit none of them.'

'But I have none more powerful than the ones already used, O warrior woman. Now you must subject me to your powers – that is, if you have any,' replied Yasi.

So Ogboinba began to utter her incantations and render her chants while at the same time she solemnly danced in a circle around her adversary. The effect was beyond belief! Now it was Yasi's turn, for his head became separated from his body and it, like Ogboinba's before, rocketed straight up into the clouds. Meanwhile, the god's body remained transfixed to the Creating Stones and Ogboinba, observing this, pushed Yasi's body down into the ground. Eventually the head returned earthward but of course it had no body to which it could attach itself, so it plummeted to the ground and was smashed to pieces. In this way the god Yasi was defeated and Ogboinba achieved yet another victory.

Eager to add the Creating Stones to her collection of mystic powers, Ogboinba decided to carry them away with her. But despite several valiant attempts to lift them, she discovered that they were impossible to move, even though they were relatively small in size. What was she to do? Who could help her? A thought came to her. She immediately began to recite a number of her incantations and spells after which she was able to pick the stones up very easily and balance them on her shoulder. Only then did she continue her journey. However, because of the extremely heavy load in her bag together with the Creating Stones she was bent double.

Ogboinba's next stop was at the kingdom of Cock. From the highest tower in his realm, Cock had been observing the overburdened traveller for some time. He flew down to her and asked if she were not the Ogboinba that the whole world, even the gods, had been talking about.

'In the entire world there is only one Ogboinba, and I am she,' came the ritual reply.

'Welcome to my kingdom,' said Cock. Please come to my palace and join me for a meal. It is such an honour to have someone as prominent as you here.'

Ogboinba was hardly in a position to refuse, so she went with Cock to his palace where she was fed a sumptuous meal befitting a royal guest. After enjoying the hospitality Ogboinba insisted that she really ought to be on her way.

'What brings you to these parts so heavy laden?' asked Cock.

'For many years now I have been married, but have been unable to bear a child. So, barren as I am, my destination is to the abode of Mother Woyengi with the request that she recreate me.'

'But this is out of the question,' cried Cock. 'You must not even attempt such a thing. Do you not know that it is impossible to see Woyengi while you are still alive? My kingdom is the last before the great void. Turn back from here or you will face disaster.'

'My mind is completely made up,' replied Ogboinba. 'Even though I am still alive, I must see Woyengi. I must keep going.'

So she took her leave of Cock and picked up her bag of mystic powers and the Creating Stones before setting off. As before, she returned after a short time and challenged Cock to a contest of powers.

'With great pleasure,' replied Cock, who enjoyed nothing better than a match of strength. He did, however, give the following warning to Ogboinba: 'The reputation I have for my powers is very wide indeed. Everyone fears me and trembles at my coming. For I am the ruler of the first and the last kingdom of things that die. Come and I shall show you my mystic powers. See if you dare to compete with me.'

After this boast, Cock flew up high to the roof of his medicine hut and began crowing a warlike song. In this way he summoned his powers. Then he returned to Ogboinba and said, 'Please begin; let me see what strength you possess.' But, as usual, Ogboinba refused to be the first and insisted that her opponent start the proceedings. Cock was not prepared to argue so he let forth with all that he possessed.

Straightaway Ogboinba was deprived of all her remedies and powers. Cock was thoroughly delighted and continued to brag: 'Mine is the first and the last kingdom of things that die. What makes you think that you can withstand my powers?' While he was still speaking, Ogboinba began to rehearse her own incantations and through chant and dance she was able to regain all of her mystic powers. She called out to Cock: 'Try again. This time with all of your powers. Omit none of them.'

'But I have no more powers to use,' replied Cock. 'Now it is your turn to do any better, if you can.' When Ogboinba repeated her spells and incantations, Cock's kingdom was suddenly enveloped by flames and burned to cinders.

With still more mystic powers in her bag, Ogboinba travelled from Cock's city and realm, the last kingdom of things that die, to that enormous field with the gigantic Iroko tree and its large supporting trunks. Finding a comfortable space in one of the trunks, our wayfarer hid herself and surveyed the scene.

In a short while a group of men and women appeared in couples from the sides of the field. Each woman held a broom and each man carried a bag. The women began sweeping the field while their partners collected the dirt into their bags. When the area had been swept clean the workers disappeared back into the sides of the field, two by two.

Ogboinba waited motionless, and as she waited the sky clouded over and darkened. All of a sudden a large table descended on to the field, followed by a chair and a huge Creation Stone. Lightning flashed and thunder boomed as if to announce the coming of Woyengi herself who alighted from above, sat on the chair, and put her feet on the Creation Stone. After this a big mound of earth materialized on the table and with it Woyengi busied herself with the process of creation. Men and women were formed and then conducted by Woyengi to two streams, the streams that flowed into the land inhabited by mankind.

Returning to the field, Woyengi commanded that the table, the chair and the Creation Stone ascend into the heavens. One by one, these three objects rose into the sky. And when the goddess herself prepared to rise with them, Ogboinba rushed out from her hiding place in the tree trunk and challenged Woyengi to a contest of powers. To this Woyengi spoke the following words: 'Did you believe that I was unaware of your presence in the Iroko tree?

I have been following your journey ever since you left your husband and home. I was there when you defeated the champions and gods on your way to find me. For it was I who gave you the mystic powers with which you gained the victories.

'So it is children that your heart desires. This is what has brought you all this way. And now you challenge me to a contest. How remarkable that you have come to the very one who gave you whatever powers you possessed! O foolish Ogboinba! I now command that all the powers that you acquired on your journey be returned to their rightful owners!'

As soon as Woyengi pronounced these words, Isembi, Egbe, the Ocean, Tortoise, the gods Ada and Yasi, and finally Cock were given all of their mystic powers back. Ogboinba was devastated. Panic struck her heart and fear overcame her. She fled far from the face of Woyengi and tried to hide. The only place she could find to escape Woyengi's wrath was in the eyes of a pregnant woman that happened to cross her path.

Now Woyengi had long ago made a solemn promise, namely, that a pregnant woman would come to no harm. Thus, since she could not injure Ogboinba, the goddess instead departed from that place and went back to her dwelling in the sky. As for Ogboinba, she did not move from her hiding place and there in the pregnant woman's eyes she has remained. But not only there. She lives in the eyes of all men and women. Have you not noticed someone looking straight at you when you gaze into someone's eyes? That is Ogboinba.

The Sheep God

A Wapangwa story (Tanzania)

At the beginning of time there was only the sky: large, clear, white and very empty. Not even the stars and the moon graced its expansive surface. There was, however, a single tree which stood upright in the air; and there was also the whirling wind. How did this tree live? Its mother and sustainer was the atmosphere. That same tree, too, was the source of life for a colony of ants, ants as white as the snow. They depended on nothing else but the suspended tree for their survival.

Wind, tree ants and atmosphere were, in turn, controlled by the efficacy of the Word. This Word was invisible and intangible. It was a dynamic force that gave one thing the power to create something else.

Very often the flight of the wind was interrupted by the presence of the tree, so it decided to get rid of the obstacle by blowing it out of the way. The wind blew and blew with all its strength until one of the tree's branches snapped off and was carried away. On it were the white ants. For quite some time this branch glided along in the air current, but eventually it slipped away from the current and hurtled downwards.

If it were not for the leaves on the branches, the ants would surely have starved to death; but after some time the insects realized that their food supply was running out. They then decided to consume all of the remaining leaves at once except for one large one. This one they used to hold their excrement; but they ate up all the others. In time, their excrement grew into an enormous mound.

When they had no more food left, the ants began to eat their own excrement and then make more and more. The ants kept on chewing and chewing until the mound was twice its original size; and they continued to re-chew and re-digest until they had created a huge mountain of excrement. Now this mountain kept on growing until it began to come close to the original tree that was suspended upright in the air. Eventually, the mountain rested on the tree and in that way the ants had more than enough leaves for their survival. Strangely enough, however, they had gotten so used to their new food that they now preferred it to the leaves of the tree. It became impossible for them to return to their original diet. Hence they continued to chew their excrement until they had formed an enormous spherical object – the world.

Of course all of this did not happen quickly. The formation of the earth's crust was completed in slow stages and took a very long time. During the process the whirling wind beat hard against the crust with its icy breath until a very large part of the excrement hardened to stone. Naturally, many of the tree ants died while others continued to reproduce and proceed with the earth's development. In time mountains, valleys, canyons, plains, deserts and wetlands covered the earth's surface.

Now the Word decided to send a particularly icy wind to blow on the world, and a chilling, white frost appeared. This was followed by a much warmer wind which made the ice melt into water. The water level rose and rose, swelling and spreading over the earth. The swelling reached the tree and all the ants were drowned while in the meantime the land became completely flooded. No part remained dry. By now the earth had reached the size it has today and it had become an enormous lake of water.

In spite of this, the earth continued to rest on the uppermost branches of the tree. But one day one of its mountains approached certain roots of the tree and those roots pierced the earth's crust. Shortly after, grass and branches began to sprout and this is how the world acquired its water, grasses and trees.

The atmosphere, too, had not been idle in the formation of living creatures on the earth. It ushered forth beings that circled around in the air, and others that crawled on the grass and ground. These beings could speak, cry out and sing; each had its own particular voice and way of using it. They became the first birds, animals and humans, and they had the ability to communicate with the other members of their species. Some remained aloft in the sky, while others settled on the earth.

But there was a shortage of food. At first the animals sought to eat the primordial tree, but the humans prevented them from doing this. The animals, however, rebelled, and attempted to eat the tree. So to punish them for their disobedience, the humans gathered all the beasts into a wide valley and began a fierce battle, using sticks and stones as weapons.

It was a mighty battle – such that the whirling wind blew with all its power and the waters were troubled. There were very many deaths and casualties. At its end, some of the animals were captured by the humans but many others escaped into the woods and forests. From there the animals began to attack and to eat people. All kinds of evil entered the world: the taking of life, cannibalism and kidnapping. And this became the pattern of existence for some time.

The humans realized that their numbers were decreasing rapidly as a result of the savage attacks of the animals. So they set out to stage a second great war. It was much worse than before and no war has ever been its equal. The ground itself began to shake and parts of it snapped loose. These pieces whirled furiously through the air and began to shine and glow with heat. They became the sun, the moon and the stars. Because the sun piece snapped off with fire, it glowed the brightest. The moon and the stars broke off without fire or flame, but later they too began to glow through the light of the sun. The sun's rays penetrated these luminaries for they were quite thin and transparent.

When this war finally came to an end, many new objects, beings and phenomena came into existence that still survive to this present day: the gods, rain, thunder and lightning. In those times people would pray to the winds, the trees, the thunder, and to other things, especially in times of war and distress. For then people had more gods than they do today.

With the beginning of peace a woolly sheep was born. It had a long tail and a pointed horn. This sheep was so happy about the end of the war that it started to jump about, cavort and throw itself into the air. On one occasion it got carried away by the air and caught fire in the atmosphere. From then on, that fiery sheep became the cause of thunder and lightning, especially in times of heavy rain. It is held by some that this sheep finally slaughtered the Word and thus became the god of the universe. It reigned over all things: the world, the moon, the stars, rain, thunder and lightning. No other spirit was greater and mightier than the sheep god.

On occasion the sheep god came down to earth from its realm in the sky, in order to stage combat with some of the gigantic trees that had not been cut down or burned during the two great wars. These trees, called Makhalati, Mpombokenzi and Mlanjzi, are the worst enemies of the sheep, and the god is always defeated by one of them.

At one time the sheep god sent lightning to strike a Mlanjzi tree and tried to destroy it. And when the sheep lowered its head in order to uproot the tree with its horns, all it could do was split the trunk and its head simply poked through on the other side. Reacting immediately, the tree quickly cut off the sheep's long tail. This was a lesson for the sheep god and from then on it has never attempted to destroy a Mlanjzi tree. Rather, it goes about killing other trees and destroying the houses that belong to those who refuse to worship it.

Some lesser gods also lived in the trees. One day, a certain man who honoured such a tree god invented a potion that had the power to attract distant objects and bring them nearer to him. The man went looking for two solid and fully grown Mlanjzi trees that were growing side by side. The man found a pair and anointed them with the potion. Soon after, the sheep god commanded the rains to fall and it wandered through the skies carrying with it the thunder and lightning. When the sheep god came close to the Mlanjzi trees, it was attracted to the medicine and dashed itself against them. In a furious rage, the god spat out fire and roared with anger. It vainly attempted to break through the trees, but as before, it only succeeded in getting its head stuck in one of them. And there the sheep stood: its head poking out one side and its body out of the other. For two whole days it remained like this, while the rains it had summoned beat down upon it. Eventually, after much strain and effort, the sheep freed itself. And until this very day, in Ubenan, Ukinga and Upangwa, where this took place, lightning can no longer destroy a Mlanjzi tree.

Before the two wars people did not believe in the gods. But after the wars things were very different. Many gods sent punishments to men and women. At one time, a group of men approached a tree god in order to ask him when the wars would end and whether he could terminate them. The tree god gave the following reply: 'For your impertinence in asking help from the elements, I shall punish you. This will teach you not to do this again. Do you agree to be punished?'

'Please do not punish us,' the men cried. 'What wrong did we do? We only came to you for assistance.'

'You kept a sheep,' the tree god replied. 'You staged wars and your sheep became insane. It threw itself into the air like an idiot and killed the Word. This Word was the cause of all beautiful things in the world. Indeed, I am the younger brother of the Word. Listen to what I have to say. Once you were wise, powerful and tall creatures. But because of the disgrace that you have brought, you shall diminish in size. Smaller and smaller will you become until in the end your height will not even be the half of what it is today. At the end of time your entire world will be consumed by fire.'

The Two Brothers

A Bantu myth (the Ambundu of Angola)

Ngunza Kilundu was travelling far from home when, in a dream, he was informed that his younger brother, Maka, was dead. On his return he inquired of his mother: 'What death was it that killed my brother Maka?'

'It was the Lord Kalunga that killed him,' was her only reply.

'If that is so, I shall go out and fight this Lord Kalunga,' said Ngunza Kilundu.

At once he went to a blacksmith and instructed him to make him a strong iron trap. When it was ready he took it out into the forest and set it, while he himself hid in the bushes armed with many weapons. Very soon he heard a miserable wail; it sounded as if some creature were in great distress. Acting on the side of caution, Ngunza Kilundu did not move out of hiding immediately. Instead he listened attentively and was surprised to detect the sounds of human speech: 'I am dying, dying!' It was the Lord Kalunga himself who had been caught in the trap, and taking aim, Ngunza Kilundu prepared to hurl his spear.

'Do not kill me!' cried out the voice. 'Come and free me!'

'Who are you,' asked Ngunza Kilundu, 'that I should set you free?'

'I am the Lord Kalunga,' came the reply.

'Ah, you are the one who killed my younger brother Maka!'

Lord Kalunga understood full well the threat that was left unsaid, and went on to explain himself.

'Do not so easily accuse me of destroying people's lives. I do not kill without motive or need for this would be of no great satisfaction for me. On the contrary, people are brought to me by their own fellow men, or through their own fault. You shall shortly see this for yourself. As for now, take your leave and wait for four days; on the fifth you may go and fetch your brother who now resides in my realm.'

Ngunza Kilundu did as he was told, and eventually made his way to the kingdom of Kalunga by the following means. After digging a deep grave near the fireplace in the earthen floor of his home, he stepped inside it and asked his mother to cover the orifice with soil. He also instructed her to water the grave every day until his return. In the underworld, Ngunza Kilundu followed a road that opened up in front of him. It led directly to the throne of Lord Kalunga who graciously received the visitor and invited him to take his place beside him.

Shortly afterwards a group of individuals began to file into the room. Lord Kalunga asked the first man, 'How did you come to die?'

'During my life,' replied the man, 'I was very rich and my neighbours were very jealous. They cast spells on me and bewitched me. They even accused me falsely of involvement in witchcraft; thus did I die.'

The next to arrive was a woman who admitted that vanity had been the cause of her death. In other words she was proud and vainglorious, overfond of riches and finery, a flirt. In the end she had been killed by her jealous husband. And so it went on: one after the other came with more or less the same story, and finally Lord Kalunga said, 'You can see for yourself what the situation is, it is not I who takes people's lives; they are simply brought to me for one or another reason. Indeed it is extremely unfair to blame one individual. Now you may go and fetch your brother from the shadows of Milunga.'

Ngunza Kilundu did as he was instructed and sought out his brother. He was surprised and delighted at finding Maka just as he had left him at their home, and obviously leading much the same sort of life as he had on earth. They greeted each other very warmly with deep embraces, and then Ngunza Kilundu said, 'Now let us get away from here, for I have come to take you home.'

'I will not go back; I do not want to set foot out of here. Things are much better for me now than they ever were while I was alive,' replied Maka much to the surprise of his brother.

'If I come back with you,' he continued, 'will I have as good a time?' Ngunza Kilundu was at a loss to answer this, so, most reluctantly, he was obliged to leave his brother where he was. Very sadly, he turned to depart but first he went to take his leave of Lord Kalunga. The noble lord saw his great disappointment and so gave him a parting present: the seeds of all the useful plants now cultivated in Angola. And then he said, 'In eight days time I shall come to visit you at your home.'

Just as he had said, Lord Kalunga came to Ngunza Kilundu's home on the eighth day only to discover that the young man had fled inland towards the rising sun. Kalunga pursued him from place to place and after great difficulty he caught up with him.

'Why are you following me,' asked Ngunza Kilundu. 'You cannot kill me; I have done nothing to deserve death. Is this not what you yourself said: that you never kill anyone? That people are brought to you through some fault of their own?' A devious smile curled on Lord Kalunga's upper lip and, saying nothing, he threw his hatchet at the imploring Ngunza Kilundu. And the young man immediately turned into a river spirit.

Stories of Obatala
Yoruba (Nigeria)

The Formation of Land

In the beginning there was no world, only a vast area of water. Then Olodumare, the supreme god, sent Obatala down from heaven to create dry land. Obatala descended on a chain and with him he carried a snail shell filled with earth, some pieces of iron and a cock. At a certain point he stopped his descent, placed the iron on the water, spread the earth from the snail shell over it and perched the cock on top. The bird straightaway began to scratch and thus the land spread far and wide.

This was how the land was formed. Eventually other spirits from heaven came down in order to inhabit it and to be with Obatala.

The Origin of Man

Obatala formed humanity from earth. He gave shape and characteristics to men and women but it was Olodumare who needed to blow into them the breath of life.

One day Obatala drank some palm wine and afterwards he formed many hunchbacks, cripples, albinos and blind persons. From that day all hunchbacks, cripples and other deformed people have been sacred to Obatala. However, his worshippers are forbidden from drinking palm wine.

It is Obatala who is responsible for giving shape to the newly-conceived child in its mother's womb.

The Destruction of Obatala

To begin with there was only one spirit in the world and this was Obatala. Obatala had a slave whom he loved well and who was his most faithful servant. But one day the slave made a request.

'Give me a farm,' he said. And Obatala gave him a patch of land. The slave established his farm and also built himself a small house at the foot of a hill. Occasionally, Obatala came and rested in his slave's house but unfortunately Obatala did not realize how evil an individual this slave was. The wicked slave planned to put an end to his master.

One day, when this villainous slave happened to observe Obatala, handsomely attired in his white gown, coming towards the farmhouse, he took to a high hill and concealed himself. As Obatala came nearer, the slave rolled a huge rock on top of his master and Obatala was smashed into hundreds of pieces.

News of this catastrophe spread far and wide. Then Orunmila, the god of the oracle, went out to the hillside and gathered up as many of the pieces as he could. Altogether he was able to collect about one half. These he put into a calabash and named it 'The Mighty Spirit'. From that time onwards there have been hundreds of lesser spirits in the world.

Obatala Reveals a Secret

On a warm summer's day Obatala went to bathe in the river but before doing so he removed his eyes and eye sockets and placed them on the river bank. While he was in the river, Eshu, the dark spirit, came and took away the eyes and the eye sockets. When Obatala returned to the bank he grew very desperate. For without his sight he could not carry out his sacred duty of forming humans.

Then the goddess Oshun came to the rescue.

'You must promise me one thing and I shall bring back your eyes and eye sockets,' she said. Obatala promised and Oshun bewitched Eshu with the grace and charm. He gave her the eyes, but before handing them over to Obatala, she said, 'Remember your promise, Obatala. I shall only return your eyes if you teach me the secret of divinity with the sixteen cowrie shells.' Obatala was displeased with this request, but what could he do? He had to reveal the secret.

Obatala and Shango

'It is high time that I went and visited my friend, Shango,' thought Obatala. As usual, before setting out, he went and consulted the oracle.

'Go not to your friend Shango,' warned the Babalawo, or a great misfortune will befall you. The signs are very bad; they even indicate the possibility of death.'

In spite of this Obatala insisted on going.

'I must go to see Shango; it has been far too long since our last meeting.'

'If that is the case, make a sacrifice to avoid certain death,' recommended the Babalawo. 'Even so,' he added, 'you will have to face much suffering. My advice to you is neither to protest under any circumstances nor to retaliate. Otherwise you will not survive the journey.'

With this, Obatala set out for Shango's kingdom. On the way, he met up with Eshu, the dark spirit, who was sitting by the roadside holding a pot full of oil.

'It is good that you are passing this way, Obatala,' cried Eshu. 'I need some help. Can you lift this pot of oil onto my head?' Obatala obliged, but as he raised the pot, Eshu poured the oil over the god. Remembering the words of the Babalawo, Obatala made no word of complaint. Instead he went down to the river and bathed himself. Eshu's plan had not worked, so he repeated his trick three times, but still Obatala did not utter a single word of complaint.

Obatala continued his journey and as he came to Shango's realm, the god saw his friend's horse come galloping towards him. Obatala captured the runaway beast, but suddenly Shango's servants turned up and, without asking any questions, mistook Obatala for the thief. Obatala was seized and thrown into prison where he was held for seven long years.

During this period, famine and destitution spread throughout Shango's kingdom. The harvest was poor, women could not bear children, and the wells dried up. Finally, Shango went to consult the oracle priest and heard the following: 'An innocent old man, captured by your servants for a crime that he did not commit, is languishing in your prison. Release him at once and all will be well.'

When Shango investigated the situation, he discovered that the old prisoner was none other than his great friend Obatala. Shango released him at once, gave him new clothes, a ring, many gifts, and made him a royal feast.

The Distant Sky

A Bini story (Nigeria)

To begin with, the sky and the earth were very near each other. Because of this, men did not need to cultivate the ground since, whenever they felt hungry, all they needed to do was to break off a piece of blue sky and eat it. Now men and women were frequently very greedy and they would cut off a lot more than what was necessary to satisfy their hunger. This made the sky extremely angry. And to add insult to injury, any left-over sky was simply thrown onto the rubbish heap. One thing was for certain, the sky did not want any of its parts to be thrown on the rubbish heap, and so he issued the following warning to humans: 'If in the future you are not careful about how you treat me, I will remove myself far from here.' This warning made everyone very nervous because they understood the consequences if the sky were no longer within reach.

For a time all men and women paid close attention to this warning. One day, however, a very greedy woman chopped off an enormous piece of the sky. She ate as much of it as she could, but of course it was far too big for her to finish it. She grew quite frightened and called for her husband to help her. But he, too, could only consume so much. A lot was left over. So together they called the entire village and even some neighbouring villages to provide assistance in eating the big piece of sky. But they too could not finish all of it.

Finally they were obliged to throw the remains on the rubbish heap. This infuriated the sky greatly and to punish the greed and waste, he soared high above the earth, far beyond the grasp of men. And from that time on, men have had to work the land for their food.

Tortoises, Humans and Stones

A *Nupe story* (*Nigeria*)

The tortoise, mankind and stones were, in the beginning, created by the high god. They each were created both male and female. On mankind and to the tortoises the god bequeathed the breath of life but not to the stones. None of them could beget children, but when they aged they were not subject to death but their youth was renewed.

Originally, the tortoise, too, could not beget children and he was very sad. So he visited the high god and expressed his wish to have offspring. But the god said, 'To you I have breathed the breath of life, but I have not granted you the possibility of begetting children.'

Disappointed by this response, the tortoise waited a little while and then paid a second visit to the high god. He expressed the same wish. Finally the god said, 'Why do you persist in asking for children? Do you not know that when the living have given birth to several children they must die?'

So the tortoise said, 'Grant me this wish, O Lord. Let me see my children and then take from me my life.' So the god granted him his wish.

Now when mankind saw the tortoise rejoicing in his offspring, he too wanted to beget children. God issued the same warning to man as he had to the tortoise: 'To you I have breathed the breath of life, but I have not granted you the possibility of begetting children. Do you not know that when the living have given birth to several children they must die?'

But the man also said, 'Grant me this wish, O Lord. Let me see my children and then take from me my life.' So the god granted him his wish.

This is how death and children came into the world. Only the stones did not desire to beget children, and for this they never die.

The Quarrel Between Earth and Sky

This Yoruba story is one of several from Western Nigeria to explain why the sky became separated from the earth. In many cultures it was thought that the earth and sky were originally together. The story also tells us how the vulture's head became bald. As in many African stories, drought and famine play a key role.

Long ago, Earth and Sky were close friends. In those days the sky and the earth were always close to one another, not like now, when the sky stays far above the earth.

Earth and Sky used to do things together. They particularly liked to go hunting. All day long they would wander in search of game, enjoying one another's company. They looked upon one another as companions and equals – they never quarrelled.

One day they went into the bush to hunt as usual. They followed the trails of antelope and deer, they tracked the wild pigs, they looked for birds, but they didn't succeed in finding anything. As the day wore on they got hungry, and they both became irritable. Just as the sun was sinking, weary with the day's exertions, they finally managed to catch a bush rat. It was not much to feed two hungry hunters, but it was the best they had. They lit a fire and roasted the bush rat. But when it was ready to eat, an argument broke out. Earth spoke.

'I will eat the first portion, because I am senior to you. In the beginning, Earth was here before Sky came into existence.'

'That's not true! Sky was here long before Earth was formed.

Therefore I should be given the first portion.'

They argued heatedly, neither giving in to the other, and as they argued they became more and more bitter. At last Sky became offended.

'This is no way to treat me. You aren't my friend any more, so why should I be yours? I don't want your company any longer. Keep your bush rat – I hope you enjoy it!' And Sky stormed off. He went high up, far above the earth and stayed there. Earth was angry too, and left the place, leaving the bush rat lying there uneaten.

Before this happened, when Earth and Sky were close, rains were plentiful, rivers were always full and the earth was always fertile. Vegetables and green things grew, the bush was abundant with game, the people's crops flourished and their harvest was good. All creatures lived an easy life. But now that Sky was far away the rains became scarce, the rivers dried up, the earth turned dry and desert spread everywhere. Wells were dried up and crops failed. The animals of the bush began to die out, and people began to starve.

A meeting was called of all the creatures of the bush to see what could be done. The dead bush rat which had been the cause of all the trouble was brought before them. They decided to appease Sky. A messenger should be chosen to carry the bush rat to Sky as a present, and beg Sky to come back down near Earth. The birds were asked to select one of their own to carry the gift. One of them was chosen, but he was unable to carry the bush rat high enough to reach Sky. Another one tried and also failed. All the strongest fliers among the birds were sent one after another, but none of them were strong enough to carry the bush rat to Sky. At last Vulture spoke.

'I can fly higher than any of you. Let me carry the bush rat to Sky.'

The other creatures laughed.

'If our best fliers can't do it, how do you suppose you will?'

But Vulture insisted, and since everyone else had tried they gave him the bush rat to carry. As he flew up towards the sky, Vulture sang.

> Earth and Sky went hunting,
> Killed a bush rat for their meal.
> Earth claimed he was senior
> But Sky did not agree.
> Sky went far up high above
> Then Earth became quite dry.
> Yams stopped growing in the fields
> And maize lost all its grains.
> Mothers searched for water
> While their babies cried with thirst.

As Vulture sang this song, flying higher and higher, Sky heard him. Sky was sorry at what was happening and decided to forget his anger. He accepted the gift of the bush rat from Vulture and in return gave Vulture a bag of magic red powder. Sky explained to Vulture that whenever rain was needed, he had only to scatter a tiny amount of this magic powder in the air, and rain would fall in abundance.

Vulture gladly took the bag of magic powder and began his long descent back down to earth. On the way, however, he felt curious to see the powder, and couldn't stop himself opening the bag to have a look. Suddenly a gust of wind blew the red powder everywhere, scattering all of it into the air at once. Instantly the light faded, big black clouds covered the sun and strong winds whipped up. The powerful winds broke the trees and blew down the houses. Then torrents of rain came crashing down and great floods surged across the land washing away crops and villages and leaving behind them devastation.

When the storm finally blew over, the creatures of the earth looked for Vulture everywhere to ask him what had happened. At last they found him. He told them about his meeting with Sky, and the magic red powder he had been given. Then he explained his unfortunate accident. They were very cross with him. They attacked him and beat him severely around the head. As a result

Vulture, who formerly had a beautiful set of head feathers, got a bald head, which he has had ever since. They were still angry with him, however, so ever since then the vulture has not been welcome amongst other animals. He has had to live apart from them and is not allowed to share their food. He always has to wait until they are finished before he can eat their left-overs.

Fam, the First Man

A *Fang* Story (*Gabon*)

Before all things began nothing at all existed – neither humans nor beasts nor vegetation. Not even the heavens or the earth existed – there was simply nothing. Nothing, that is, except the great god Nzame. He was. Now Nzame was three, and his names were Nzame, Mebere and Nkwa.

Nzame was the creator of the heavens and the earth. He chose to dwell in the heavens, high above his creation. With his powerful breath, Nzame blew onto the earth and both dry land and water were made, each keeping to one side of the other.

Nzame then created everything else: the sun, moon, stars, beasts, birds, vegetation; absolutely everything. And when he had completed all that we see today, he called Mebere and Nkwa to show them his handiwork.

'This is my creation. Do you approve?'

'Yes, you have done very well,' they replied.

'Have I omitted anything?' he asked. With one voice, Mebere and Nkwa replied. 'Of course we see great beauty and much variety. However, although we see many animals, who is their leader? We see much vegetation, but who is its master?'

So it was decided that the elephant, the leopard and the monkey be given dominion over all things. They chose the elephant because it was a very wise beast; and the leopard because it was strong and shrewd; and the monkey because it could discern and was versatile.

But Nzame wanted to make something that was even more superior than these three animals. So with the help of Mebere and Nkwa he produced a creature almost like themselves. Nzame gave him power, Mebere gave him agility, and Nkwa gave him beauty. Then all three, as if with one voice, spoke to the new creature, saying: 'Possess the earth. From now on you are to rule over all that is. Life is within you, as it is within us. All things are yours. You are the lord and master.'

This accomplished, Nzame, Mebere and Nkwa returned to their celestial dwelling place, leaving the new being to remain below alone as lord of all. Everything did homage to him and obeyed him. Nevertheless among all the beasts, the elephant remained the first in rank, the leopard the second, and the monkey the third, out of respect for the original choice of Mebere and Nkwa.

Nzame, Mebere and Nkwa called the new creature Fam, meaning strength. Fam was the first man. But it did not take long before Fam became proud because of his superior gifts. He was proud of his power; he was proud of his agility; and he was proud of his beauty. Neither the elephant nor the leopard nor the monkey could excel him in any of these qualities. There was no living creature that he could not subdue. Evil entered man's heart, and arrogance too. In fact, Fam decided that he would no longer worship Nzame, and he rebuked the god with this scornful song:

Yeye, o, layeye,
Nzame rules on high,
Man rules on earth,
Yeye, o, layeye,
God is for god,
Man is for man,

Each in his domain,
Each one for himself!

Nzame heard the song and called out: 'What song is this?'
'Seek him out; seek him out,' continued the haughty Fam.
'What song is this?' repeated Nzame.
'Yeye, o, layeye; yeye, o, leyeye,' chortled the singer. 'It is I who sings, Fam the all-powerful.'
Enraged, Nzame summoned the thunder god, Nzalan. 'Do my bidding!' commanded Nzame. Nzalan's heavy stamping could be heard from a great distance as he came running towards Nzame: boom, boom, boom! 'Strike the earth below!' Flashes of fiery spears struck the ground and set the forests ablaze. The fields and plains burnt like kindling; it was a terrifying inferno which consumed all life on the face of the earth: trees, plants, fruit, nuts, beasts, fish, birds. Everything was annihilated, everything became cinder.
Now when Nzame had first made Fam, he promised him that he would be immortal. 'You will never die,' he said. And the promises of Nzame are irrevocable. But the first man was engulfed in flames and who knows what became of him? Surely he is alive, but where is he?
Nzame set his gaze over the earth, now a mass of smouldering charcoal, devoid of life; impotent. He felt sorry for what he had done and decided to rectify the situation. Nzame, Mebere and Nkwa came together in council and set out the following programme: they spread out a new layer of earth over the black expanse of ash. Almost immediately a new green shoot appeared and grew into a tree which kept on getting taller and taller. In time, a seed fell from one of the branches and a new tree was born. Leaves fell from the boughs, split into two, grew bigger and bigger, and began to walk. One leaf turned into an elephant, another into a leopard, another became a monkey, an antelope, a hare, until all the beasts appeared once more.
Other leaves drifted into water and began to float. Marine life

burst forth: here a fish, there a crab, an oyster, a prawn; until all sea life appeared once more. The earth became again what it had once been, and what it is today. And just to prove that this tale is true, you only have to dig up the earth in certain places to find particular hard black stones which can be broken into pieces. Throw these into a fire and they burn.

But one thing was missing and that was a leader. This time Nzame, Mebere and Nkwa met to discuss the matter. They did not want to make the same mistake twice. Finally they decided to make another man, just like Fam. 'Let us give him the same limbs and organs,' said Nzame, 'but this time we shall not promise total immortality. We shall turn his head so that he can see death.'

To this second man they gave the name Sekume, and he became the father of all. Nzame did not want him to be left alone, so he issued the following command: 'Make yourself a woman from a tree.' Sekume obeyed. He brought forth a help mate from a tree and named her Mbongwe.

Now Sekume and Mbongwe were created in two parts, according to the decision of Nzame. The outer part was called Gnoul, the body, and the inner part which resides in the body, was called Nsissim. Nsissim is the part that casts the shadow, and is in fact one and the same with the shadow. It is Nsissim that gives life to the soul. Only when man dies does Nsissim depart from the body. But Nsissim itself does not die. It is very easy to detect Nsissim's whereabouts because it lives in the very centre of the eye: it is the tiny, shining point that you see in the middle, that is Nsissim.

> Stars on high,
> Fire below,
> Coal in the hearth,
> The soul in the eye,
> Cloud, smoke and death.

Sekume and Mbongwe lived happily on earth and gave birth to many children. But what happened to Fam, the first man? He was imprisoned by Nzame under the earth and a large stone sealed the entrance. For years and years the evil Fam dug away at the earth from below and at long last he surfaced. What a change! 'Who has usurped my position?' cried Fam. He was extremely angry with Sekume and he waits day by day to ambush and to kill him.

> Remain silent,
> Fam hears all.
> He brings distress,
> Remain silent.

Nyambe and Kamunu

A *Malozi story (Zambia)*

Long, long ago the god Nyambe and his beautiful wife, the goddess Nasilele, dwelt on earth. Nyambe was the creator of all good things: he made the animals that live on the land, the birds that fly in the skies and the fish that dwell in the deep seas. Finally he made a man and called him Kamunu.

Now Kamunu was by far the most intelligent of all living creatures. For when Nyambe carved a piece of wood, Kamunu also carved one for himself. When Nyambe hollowed out a drinking cup, Kamunu did the same for himself. When Nyambe forged metals, the man forged too. Nyambe was astonished, and even became alarmed; he began to fear and even dread the man that he had created.

One day the man Kamunu forged himself a long, pointed spear and with it he killed the male offspring of Nyambe's favourite beast, the red antelope. Not content with this, Kamunu slaughtered other creatures as well, and ate them savagely.

In a rage, Nyambe shouted at the man, exclaiming: 'What is this that you are doing, Kamunu. Your deeds are wicked. Why do you kill? What have the animals done to offend you? What possesses you to want to eat them? Are they not your brothers? Are not all of you my children?' So Nyambe banished the man from his presence and caused him to go to a far-away country.

In that place Kamunu remained for an entire year, eating his fill, but anxious for more. So he returned to the land of Nyambe where he made a first stop by a cool stream. There he was spotted by Kangomba, the large red antelope. Totally distraught at seeing the murderer of her son, Kangomba rushed to find Sasisho, Nyambe's messenger bird.

'I saw a man down by the cool stream. In his hands are a magic pot and a club. Surely it is Kamunu, the one who used to kill the animals.' Sasisho went to Nyambe and said, 'Kamunu is here; he has returned. Kangomba saw him by the cool stream.'

'I have already been informed,' replied Nyambe quietly. 'Let him sit down.'

After a time Kangomba brought Kamunu to Sasisho, the messenger bird of Nyambe. 'Tell Nyambe that I have returned. I demand from him land to cultivate so that I will not need to kill the animals.' So Kamunu was given ten large fields; but at night a herd of buffalo trampled all over the fields. This made Kamunu furious, so he took his bow and arrows and wounded a buffalo which soon died. The following day, Kamunu went directly to Nyambe and said, 'I have killed a buffalo.'

'Eat it,' replied Nyambe.

Kamunu's pot, the one he used to mix his magic potions in, died. So Kamunu went to Kangomba, the red antelope, and said, 'Go to Nyambe for me. Tell him my magic pot has died.'

'My own things also end like that,' replied Nyambe.

Kamunu returned to his home by the fields. At night a herd of deer trampled all over his crops. This made Kamunu furious so he took his bow and arrows and wounded a male deer which soon died. So Kamunu went to Kangomba, the red antelope, carrying the tail of the deer, and said, 'Go to Nyambe for me. Tell him I have killed the deer.' Kangomba went to Nyambe, who said, 'Let him eat the tail. It will be my welcome present.'

Kamunu returned to his home by the fields and discovered that his dog had died. So Kamunu went to Kangomba, the red antelope, and said, 'Tell Nyambe my dog has died.'

'I have already been informed,' replied Nyambe. 'It is good.'

When Kamunu returned to his home by the fields, he said to his wife, 'When I visited Nyambe, I saw my magic pot and my dog.'

'This cannot be true,' replied his wife. 'It is not like that.'

That night a herd of elephants trampled on Kamunu's fields; but the man was fast asleep. His wife, however, heard the noise and woke him. 'Go to the fields,' she cried. So Kamunu, armed with his spear, went out and wounded a young elephant that soon died. In the morning he went to Kangomba, and said, 'Go to Nyambe on my behalf and tell him that I have killed a young elephant.'

'Eat it,' replied Nyambe. 'Consider this a welcome gift. Since your return to our land I have given you no present. Go ahead, eat.'

Kamunu went back to his home. He came to his wife and said, 'Nyambe instructed me to eat the elephant. He says it is our welcome gift.'

Kamunu's child died; so he went to Kangomba. 'Go to Nyambe on my behalf and speak to him. Tell him that my child is dead.'

'Come with me,' said Kangomba.

So together they went to Nyambe and there Kamunu saw his child sitting next to the god.

'My own things also end like that,' replied Nyambe.

Exasperated, Nyambe summoned a council. Sasisho and Kangomba were amongst those present.

'It is impossible to stay here any more. Kamunu can reach us far too easily. He will destroy everything.'

So they decided to go and live on an island.

But this did not deter Kamunu. He tied together a large number of logs, placed then in the sea and stood on them. Casting out, he went in search of Nyambe on his island. Kamunu also made a canoe from the trees of the forest and in it he placed an assortment of animals, birds and fish, which he presented to Nyambe. But this saddened Nyambe. He accepted the offerings but refused to eat them, for they were his children.

Then Nyambe raised up a tall mountain from the ground. On its peak he went to live and hide from the man; but even there did Kamunu follow him. Where could the god go to avoid the man? How could he flee from him? Sasisho and Kangomba searched all over the world for a place of refuge, a sanctuary. But wherever they went they met the children of men.

So they summoned the sages and magi; they summoned also the prophetic insect Simbukiki: 'Take us to the North; take us to the South,' they cried. Some of the sages and magi instructed them to send all of the fowl of the air to locate Litooma, the legendary city. But it could never be found. They then called on Nalungwana, the divine. And Nalungwana divined and said, 'O great King Nyambe, your life is in the hands of Liuyii, the spider. Use his powers to find you a place of safety.'

Liuyii was taken to Nyambe who enjoined the spider to go with Sasisho to look for a safe haven for Nyambe. After many weeks they returned and declared: 'We have at last found a town.' But Nalungwana found the place unacceptable.

'Do not go there,' he said. 'This is not the right place. The land that you want is across the river.'

So Sasisho and Liuyii crossed the river and eventually reached Litooma, the legendary city. When they returned to Nyambe and Nalungwana, they said, 'On the opposite bank of the river lies the city of Litooma; this is the right place.' Nalungwana found this completely satisfactory.

When Nyambe asked the animals if they wanted to accompany him to Litooma, where man would never harm them, they adamantly refused and came up with all sorts of excuses. Most of them declared that they could not really go and live anywhere else.

Kangomba, the red antelope, said, 'My speed shall save me; Kamunu cannot run.' The gnu said, 'I, too, can survive by speed.' The fish said, 'Why should I fear man? I live deep in the water.' The hippopotamus said, 'Man has no strength; I can kill him easily. He is much weaker than I.' The elephant said, 'The same goes for me.'

'And for us,' chimed in the buffalo and the lions. The hyena said, 'What have I to fear? I shall ambush him at night and attack him in his sleep.' The wild goose said, 'My wings will keep me away from Kamunu.'

'And us,' said the other birds. And so on; and so on.

Nyambe tried desperately to change their minds because he knew that Kamunu could trick each and every one of them. So he said, 'Listen to me, my children. Do as I command. Each and every one of you go now and collect some wood.' In an hour a large pile of wood was formed. Nyambe then said, 'Now put a flame to the wood and boil up a kettle.' The fire was lit and a great flame surged skyward. Even the nearby soil was scorched. 'Now let us see who is capable of removing the kettle from the flames.'

The gnu made an attempt, but drew back in fear. The red antelope and the deer also tried but failed. Most of the others could not even draw near to the roaring inferno, so they kept well back. A valiant attempt was made by the elephant and the rhinoceros, but their skin was burnt and they had to plunge into the river. The challenge was beyond all of them: none could lift the kettle out from the fire.

Thereupon Nyambe called Kamunu who, together with his people, went down to the river with wooden cups, calabashes and pots to fill them with water. Then they drenched the area with the river water, approached the flame, poured much water onto it until not even a spark could be seen. Then they took hold of the kettle. A man was sent to Nyambe to say: 'We have removed the kettle from the burning wood.'

Whereupon Nyambe gathered together all the men and all the

beasts and spoke these words: 'If a human child was born this day, let him be brought here. But man refused and cried: 'How can this be? A tender, newly-born babe is more of water than of flesh. No one other than his mother can hold him.'

Nyambe then said, 'If a beast gave birth this day, let the young be brought here.' Without hesitation, a newly-born kid approached and Nyambe declared, 'Let the beasts walk alone as soon as they are born. But let man sit for a year before he walks.'

Not all of the animals refused to accompany the god. The ones that agreed are those whose kind is unknown to us. They, with Nyambe, his wife Nasilele, and his messenger bird Sasisho crossed the river and, led by Liuyii the spider, entered the legendary city of Litooma. Now Nalungwana the diviner decreed, 'Let Liuyii's eyes be deprived of their sight so that he may never find his way to Litooma again. Or else he may be enticed to bring Kamunu to Nyambe.' Then Nyambe ascended into the skies, alone.

Kamunu, however, learned that Nyambe had risen into the clouds, so he called together all the people and said, 'We must build a very high tower in order to reach Nyambe.' So the people set about building a high tower. To begin with, they laid out a foundation of wooden posts, then they attached others to these, tying them together with bark twine. In due course they had constructed an enormous tower that reached into the clouds. However, the bark twine that was used to tether the wooden posts could not take the strain. So the tower collapsed to the ground killing the workers at the top.

Then did Kamunu cease his efforts to search out Nyambe. But every morning, with the rising of the sun, he called out: 'Behold our king! He has appeared!' And bending his forehead to the ground, with hands clasped together he uttered the following prayer: Mangue, mangue Mulyete! ('Glory, glory, glory to the one above!').

From that time forth, when man sets out to hunt, or when he dreams a dream, or when he is sick, he entreats Nyambe with humility, and offers the god water in a wooden goblet. And on those days which are holy days he will do no work. At the setting of the sun, man again prostrates himself in adoration. Furthermore, he also venerates Nasilele, Nyambe's consort, especially when the moon is new. And when he is buried, man is placed in a grave with his face towards the east, so that he may know how to come to Nyambe. Upon his arrival at the bank of the river, man is received by Nyambe – but only if he possesses ritual markings on his arms and holes in his ear lobes – and shown the path that leads to the king. There man will live without want.

When a woman is buried, she is placed in her grave with her face towards the east, so that she may know how to come to Nasilele. But if neither the man nor the woman has the ritual markings on the arms or holes in their ear lobes, they will end up as food for the worms. Or else they must travel along the cruel and dangerous road which becomes narrower and narrower until it ends altogether in the hideous wilderness where they will suffer from hunger and thirst until they meet their doom.

2
The Elements and Celestial Powers

Father Moon

A Wakaranga story (Zimbabwe)

When the Great Spirit created a man, he called him Moon. Now at first Moon lived in the depths of the sea. Moon was lonely and bored; he wanted to go and live on the earth but the Great Spirit would have nothing of this. 'I warn you, O Moon, life on earth is extremely arduous, and you will regret ever having left the sea.' But Moon persisted and pleaded so that finally the Great Spirit gave in and set him on the face of the earth.

The change from sea to land did not alleviate Moon's loneliness. In fact, Moon soon discovered himself on a barren and uninhabited expanse of desert. There were neither trees nor flowers, nor any living creatures. At least on the sea bed he had had plants and marine life to look at. Moon was most unhappy and cried bitterly to the Great Spirit. 'You did not heed my warning,' said the Spirit, 'and now look at you! Nevertheless, I shall take pity on you and give you a help mate. For two years you shall have the company of a wife. Her name will be Morningstar.'

The Elements and Celestial Powers

Thus Morningstar came to dwell with Moon. Her home had been in the heavens where she was clothed in fire and light. (These were the two gifts that she brought with her to earth.) Moon took his new wife to his hut and at night when she lay down to sleep, Morningstar lit a fire and reclined on one side of it. Moon slept on the other side. But during the night Moon walked through the flames and lay close to Morningstar.

The following morning Moon saw that his wife's body had become immensely swollen. And in time Morningstar gave birth to all species of vegetation: trees, grasses, plants, flowers, reeds and bushes. Eventually the entire world was clothed in a rich, green garment. Some of the trees began to grow extremely tall, so tall in fact that they got higher and higher until they reached the clouds.

As soon as the trees touched the sky the clouds burst open with rain. The grateful land produced an abundance of fruit, vegetables, roots and seeds. How happy Moon and Morningstar were! Theirs was a life of plenty.

It was not long before the two years came to an end. The Great Spirit kept his word and summoned Morningstar away from her husband placing her once again in the sky. Moon, utterly forlorn, wept bitterly for eight days. This time the Great Spirit provided Moon with a second help mate to ease his loneliness. 'She will live with you for two years, but at the end of that time you must die. Her name is Eveningstar.'

So Eveningstar went and dwelt with Moon for two years, as the Great Spirit had prescribed. After the first night's sleep, Moon discovered to his amazement that his new wife's belly had swollen up. And in time Eveningstar gave birth to all kinds of animal life: goats, sheep and cows on one day; antelopes and birds on the next; and boys and girls on the third day.

On the fourth day, Moon again wished to sleep with Eveningstar, but the Great Spirit said, 'Let things remain as they are for the hour of your death approaches.' But Moon did not hearken to the Great Spirit and defiantly slept a fourth night with his wife.

The next morning Eveningstar's body had swollen up as before, but this time she gave birth to dangerous and vicious beasts: lions, leopards, snakes and scorpions. And the Great Spirit said, 'You did not heed my warning and now look at what has happened.'

Now Moon looked upon his daughters and seeing that they were beautiful, he desired them. They gave birth to many, many children, and he, as their father, became king of a large realm. But Eveningstar became jealous of her daughters and she sent a snake to bite Moon and fill him with poisonous venom. Once bitten, Moon fell extremely ill. At the same time many other strange events occurred. For example, the clouds did not shed their rain upon the earth, thus the lakes and the rivers began to dry up; the vegetation began to wither and there was a great famine over the land.

Moon's children searched for a means to bring rain down upon the earth. They said to each other, 'This is all the fault of our father, Moon.' So they attacked their father by the throat until he could no longer breathe, cast him into the deep sea, and set up another man as their ruler.

But Moon rose from the sea; for he caught sight of his first love, Morningstar, and until today he pursues her across the night sky. For he remembers how happy they were together.

Morning and Evening

A Fon story (Dahomey)

Even though Morning and Evening were brothers, their father, Mahu, the high god, did not treat them the same way. Morning was born first, and on him Mahu showered presents, riches and many, many subjects. Evening, the second brother, merely received a calabash with two kinds of beads – nana and azamun – the only two things that his father had not given to Morning.

One day Morning became extremely ill. A doctor was called and after examining him said that two items were needed to cure Morning: a nana bead and an azamun bead. Immediately, Morning's subjects searched far and wide for the beads, but none were to be found. Finally, they discovered that Evening had what they were looking for.

'What price will you pay me for these precious stones?' asked Evening.

'Two hundred cowries for both beads,' they replied. So Evening gave them two beads and in time Morning was cured.

After a while Evening began to do some serious thinking. He even began to hope that the same illness would strike his brother many more times so that he could acquire a great store of cowries. Then he recalled that whenever Morning approached, the leaves of the calabash rolled up and shut themselves tightly. So the next time he made certain that only open calabash leaves would fall under Morning's feet. In this way the older brother straightaway fell ill. Evening now was able to strike his brother with this illness as often as he liked. Eventually Morning's entire collection of cowries became his own.

It was not long before Morning's subjects began to leave him and chose to gather around Evening whom they now considered as their king. Evening was given twelve pages for an escort.

The Sun, the Moon and the Creation of Fish

A Fon story (Dahomey)

When the sun first made his appearance in the sky, he was surrounded by his many children, much as the moon is surrounded at night. But there was a very big difference. For the sun and his family produced an overwhelming amount of heat. It was so unbearably hot that the people on the face of the earth could scarcely go out from their huts. It was almost impossible to gather or to look for food during the day. Life was a misery and everyone was totally dissatisfied.

Seeing this, the moon decided to give some friendly advice to the sun. She had a plan.

'Our children, both yours and mine, are causing a great deal of distress,' said the moon. 'All men and women are complaining about them. Let us do something about this difficult situation. I suggest that we gather our children into sacks and throw them into the sea.'

Now the moon, instead of putting her children into a sack, placed white pebbles instead. The sun, knowing nothing of this, put all of his children into a sack and followed the moon to the sea where they tossed their loads into the water.

That night, the sun observed that the moon was still surrounded by all of her children. He was furious, and said, 'You deceiver! Tomorrow I shall retrieve all of my children from the sea!'

But when the sun drew one of his children from the water, it died immediately. The next also died, as did the next. The others, below the surface of the sea, still shone as before, but they could no longer see their father. And the sun, fearing that he might destroy all of them, left them to live in the sea.

From that time onwards, the sun has despised the moon. He chases her every day. On some occasions he actually catches her.

Thunder and Lightning

(*Source unknown*)

When the world was first created both Thunder and Lightning dwelt among men and women on dry land. In fact, both of them were beasts: Thunder was an elderly mother sheep and Lightning, her only son, was a strong, handsome ram. But neither of them had many friends. Indeed, when the young ram, Lightning, was slighted by any human being or other animal, he would fly into a furious rage and begin destroying houses and fields. He was so strong that he could even uproot large trees or damage an entire harvest. Even people who got in his way were known to have been killed.

As soon as his mother, Thunder, discovered that he was acting so rashly and cruelly, she would lift up her voice and bellow with all her might. The sound that she could produce was actually very alarming.

Inevitably, the townspeople were extremely distraught at this kind of behaviour. First there was the damage caused by Lightning to property and land and then the intolerable commotion that always followed the ram's frenzied outbursts. The people frequently addressed the ruler with their complaints until he could tolerate the situation no longer. Finally he commanded the two of them to take up their abode at the very far end of the town. It was prohibited for them to have any dealings at all with the townsfolk.

This restriction, however, was not particularly effective since Lightning could still observe people as they walked about the town's streets and it was very easy for him to go up to them and pick a quarrel. The ruler was thus obliged to summon mother and son again.

'You have been given ample opportunity to improve your way of life,' said the ruler, 'but it is obvious that you make no attempt to do so. For this reason I am forced to banish you altogether from this town. From this time forth you must find a place to live in the distant forest. Do not show your faces here again.'

Thunder and Lightning were scarcely in a position to disobey the ruler's command. So they left the town in a very foul mood, cursing and insulting the inhabitants all the while. In an act of violent revenge, Lightning set fire to the entire forestland. This had particularly disastrous consequences because it happened to be the dry season and the townsfolk were to face more trouble than ever before.

The flames swept along the parched land and consumed the small gardens and orchards that the people had planted. In some places the fire even reached the houses, causing loss of precious shelter. Everyone was in a state of panic. And even though one could frequently hear the mother ram's powerful voice calling her son to order, it made no difference at all to his wicked intentions.

The ruler summoned all his advisers together and asked for their suggestions as to how to put an end to this misery. Finally, after much deliberation, they came up with a strategy. One of the group, an elderly man known for his wisdom and discretion, proposed the following: 'In my opinion it would be to the benefit of all if we sent Thunder and Lightning far, far away – indeed right away from the earth. Anywhere on land where they might live will surely lead to some kind of catastrophe. They must be flung high up into the sky. Only then shall we be rid of them.' Everyone agreed that this would be the only solution to their dilemma.

So Thunder and Lightning were banished to the skies where they were exiled forever. But were the townsfolk's problems at an end? Not entirely. For Lightning still finds opportunities to lose his temper as a result of which he sends missiles of fire earthward. For this, as before, his mother continues to chastise him in her ferocious growling voice. But even she gets so exasperated with him that she has to abandon him from time to time. Everyone knows when this happens, for Lightning still hurls his fiery lances towards the earth, but his mother is so far removed that she neither hears or sees, and her reproaches are not to be heard.

A Daughter-in-law for Kimanaweze

(Bantu)

When the time came for the son of Kimanaweze to choose a wife, he proudly declared that he did not wish to marry a mere mortal woman. Rather, he would wed the royal daughter of the Sun and the Moon. To that end he prepared a written message and sought diligently for a courier to take it up to the sky. Most of the birds and animals refused: the grey eagle had better things to do, so did the red antelope and the hawk and the vulture. Finally and most unexpectedly, Mainu the frog appeared and offered to carry and to transmit the important message.

But the son of Kimanaweze doubted very much that the frog had the ability to carry out the task successfully.

'Be off with you!' he said. 'Those who have wings and an articulate voice have rejected me. How is it that you believe that you can do my bidding?'

Mainu, however, stubbornly refused to take 'no' for an answer. He persisted night and day until Kimanaweze's son gave in.

'And be prepared for the thrashing of your life if you do not succeed,' he warned the frog.

Now the Sun and the Moon were in the habit of sending their handmaidens down to the earth in order to draw water for their palace. They descended and ascended by means of a spider's web. Observing this, Mainu the frog went and hid himself in the well to which they came, and when the first handmaiden lowered her pitcher he placed the letter in his mouth and then jumped into the jar without being seen. The young ladies climbed up into the skies, carried their water pitchers into the palace, and set them down. When they went off to seek their master and mistress, the frog emerged from the water jar, brought out the letter, laid it on a table well in sight and hid.

After some time Kumbi Mwene, the Lord Sun, entered the room where the frog had concealed himself. He noticed the letter on the table and read it, but not knowing what to make of it, he simply put it away and said nothing about it. At the first available opportunity the frog jumped into an empty water jug and soon was carried down to earth again when the maids went for a fresh supply of water.

'What response do you have?' asked the son of Kimanaweze. Of course the frog had absolutely nothing to say and this made the young man highly suspicious. Had the frog carried out his responsibilities at all? Nevertheless, after several days, our hapless bridegroom composed another letter and sent the courier frog off once again. The frog carried it in the same way as before, and Kumbi Mwene, after reading it, wrote a reply.

'I consent to this proposal,' read the response, 'but it is imperative that I see exactly who my future son-in-law is. You must come to my palace yourself and bring with you the "initial gift".' This was the customary present which opened marriage negotiations.

The frog immediately brought the response to the impatient suitor and upon receiving it the young man wrote another letter with the following message: 'I am delighted and honoured to learn that you are willing to accept me as your future son-in-law. However, before I come to you I must first wait until I am informed of the kilembu.' (The kilembu was the 'wooing present' or bride price.) This he gave to the frog, along with a sum of money, and it was despatched as before.

Upon receiving this latest letter, Kumbi Mwene apprised his wife, the Moon, of the developments. She was also perfectly willing to welcome the mysterious young man into her household. Normally, at this stage in the proceedings it would have been appropriate for the future mother-in-law to provide refreshments for the diligent envoy. But owing to his invisibility, Moon solved the problem by saying, 'We shall cook a meal in any case, and leave it on the table where he places the letters.' This done, the frog, when left totally alone, came out from his hiding place and consumed the food.

A letter was left together with the fare. It stated that the amount of the kilembu would be 'a sack of money'. The frog carried the written details back to the son of Kimanaweze, who spent six busy days in collecting the necessary amount, and then sent it with the frog back to the celestial abode of the royal luminaries. He also forwarded the following communication: 'Soon I shall instruct you of the day I wish to bring home my wife.'

This, however, was more easily said than done. For when his messenger, Mainu, had once more returned, the young suitor searched for twelve days to find an escort for his noble bride. But his efforts were all in vain for he could find no one willing to do him this favour. Once more, however, the valiant frog rose to the occasion. Again he had himself carried up to the Sun's palace, and hopping out of the water jug, concealed himself in a corner of the room until after dark, when he came out and went through the palace until he located the princess's bed chamber.

Seeing that she was fast asleep, the messenger frog, who possessed magic powers, took out one of her eyes without waking her, and then the other. He tied up the eyes in a handkerchief and then went back to his hiding place in the room where the water jugs were kept. In the morning, when their daughter did not turn up for breakfast, her parents sought her out to discover the reason, only to discover that she had become blind. In their distress they sent two men to consult the diviner, who, after casting lots and not having been informed by anyone of the day's unfortunate finding, said, 'Disease has brought you. The one who is sick is a woman. The sickness that possesses her has affected her eyes. You have come to me, being sent; you have not come of your own will. I have spoken.' Kumbi Mwene's messengers replied, 'This is the complete truth. Can you tell us what has caused the ailment? Look now at your lots and speak.'

'A certain suitor has cast a spell over her,' replied the seer, 'and she will die unless she is sent to him. Thus I advise you to make haste with the marriage.'

The emissaries brought back the words of the diviner to the Sun, who said, 'Very well; let us now retire. In the morning we shall send her down to the earth.' Accordingly, on the following day, Kumbi Mwene gave orders for the spider to spin a large cobweb in order to carry his daughter down to her husband on the earth. Meanwhile, the frog had gone down as usual in the water jug and hidden himself in the bottom of the well. When the water carriers had gone up again he came out and went to the village of the bridegroom and informed him that his bride would arrive that very day. The young man found this to be totally inconceivable and refused to believe the frog.

'You have my solemn word that I shall bring her to you by the evening,' said the frog. And he returned to the well.

After dusk the attendants brought the princess down to the earth by way of the newly spun cobweb and left her by the well. The frog came out and told her that he would take her to her husband's house; at the same time he produced her eyes and re-inserted them. In due course they reached the home of the son of Kimanaweze and the marriage took place with much celebration and festivity.

The Discovery of Fire

(*Source unknown*)

In very ancient times people did not know the meaning of fire. Food was never cooked; iron was not forged; pots were not baked. All meat was eaten totally raw. One day a hunter went out into the forest to look for game. He had little luck and thus was forced to wander far from his home village. Finally he caught sight of a magnificent bird with feathers of many colours and decided to chase it. Further and further he ran into unknown parts following the swift flight of the beautiful bird until it soared completely out of sight.

'What shall I do now?' he wondered. 'Go home with empty hands or continue my hunting?' Then it occurred to him that he had strayed into completely foreign territory and even if he wanted to, he could not retrace his steps to his village. As he was pondering his plight, the hunter looked up into the distant sky and saw something that he had never seen before: a thin cloud rising straight up into the air.

'What could this be?' he asked himself. Of course it was smoke, but the hunter was at a loss to put a name to it. So he set off in the direction of this rising wisp of cloud.

It seemed to him that he had gone many miles but was getting no nearer to his destination. What the hunter did not know was that a column of smoke may climb very high into the air and be visible at a great distance. Eventually twilight fell and the sun disappeared. The hunter could no longer see the smoke, but just as he was about to abandon his search, he spotted far away a strange light below the horizon.

'How strange,' thought the hunter. 'What could this be? Is it a fallen star perhaps?' Now people who have never experienced fire know nothing about artificial light, for without fire it is impossible to burn a lamp, a candle, or a torch. The only night lights this man had seen were from the heavenly bodies but none of them had ever glowed below the horizon. So he went ahead in the direction of this extraordinary sight to find out what it was about.

As he came closer and closer, he noticed that the light, which was a flame, flickered and flashed with the brilliance of a star.

'But it is not at all like a star,' he mused. 'For sparks and tongues shoot up from it and out of it issues a swirling cloud.' Moreover, when he approached it, he noticed that the fire was full of agitation and emitted a strong heat which prevented him from touching it. The hunter concluded that this must be the manifestation of a powerful spirit. With considerable trepidation and cautious scrutiny, he walked as near as he could to the flames and spoke the following words: 'Greetings to you, great Master! The sun has now set. How do you fare?'

The fire responded to these courteous remarks in a crackling voice: 'Be welcome, O traveller! I invite you to keep me company this night. Come closer and make yourself warm. But first you must provide me with wood: trees, shrubs, trunks, dead branches, dry grass and reeds.'

Quite overcome by astonishment, the hunter set off to gather dry branches and kindling wood which he tossed onto the fire piece by piece, just as the fire had instructed him. As he fed the fire, he was surprised to notice that the flames increased in size very quickly. Indeed, the blaze grew rapidly to enormous proportions the more he added sticks and branches.

'You, yourself have need of food,' remarked the fire. 'Look behind you this very moment.' The man did so and saw a hare sitting nearby, staring into the fire as if mesmerized by its glow. Quickly he fitted an arrow into his bow and let it fly. Once he had skinned his dead prey, the hunter prepared to consume it raw, as was his custom. But the fire stopped him with the following words: 'Come here, young man, and cook your food so that you may savour its fragrance and enjoy its taste. Meat is much more delicious when it is allowed to roast.'

Never before having heard the word 'roast', the hunter had no idea how to go about it. Following further instructions from the fire, he soon learned that the most efficient way was to skewer the meat onto the blade of his spear. When he had eaten the cooked meat he vowed never again to eat meat raw. He was also determined to find a way of taking the fire back to his village with him. Light, warmth and roasting were three luxuries that he could now no longer do without. The hunter summoned up a lot of courage and made the proposition to the fire.

'I promise to keep you very well fed and to look after you for as long as I live,' said the man sincerely. However, the fire, very politely and quite firmly declined.

'It is impossible for me to travel and I fully forbid it. Such an act would be extremely dangerous not only for you, the bearer, but for all other living beings and for the natural environment. Better that I stay right here where the gods have placed me. Although you must never attempt to take me away, you are always welcome to come here as often as you wish to warm yourself, to feed me, and to roast your meat. One more thing, never tell anyone about my existence for they might seek me out and steal me.'

The man honoured the fire's wishes and that night he rested cosily near its flames. In the morning he rose refreshed and rested and bid the fire farewell.

'Goodbye to you, O fire, and thank you. I shall be glad to come back one day.'

After some difficulty, the hunter eventually located the path that led him home to his village. Upon his arrival, he gave his wife some of the roasted hare which he had so much enjoyed out in the forest. But as it turned out, this act of generosity proved to be a fatal mistake. For having tasted the succulent cooked meat, the woman asked for more. Consequently, the man was obliged to go back again and again to visit the fire. There he not only made himself comfortable and warm but also roasted meat for himself and his wife. The fire was always accommodating and indeed was happy to have the hunter's company. For his part, the hunter ungrudgingly fed the flames with dry sticks and branches. Gradually, he learned how to keep the fire burning nicely with big logs and how to rekindle it with dry leaves when he had been absent for a very long time and found it smouldering in its ashes.

In due course his wife informed a friend about her husband's long absences and the appetizing meat that he brought home. This aroused the friend's curiosity, so he decided to follow the hunter the next time he went out into the forest. He kept behind the hunter at a safe distance until he saw the wisp of rising smoke, and then the fire. As darkness fell the spy crept up closer and closer to see what the hunter was up to. Following his usual routine, the hunter placed branches and logs on the fire before settling down for the night's sleep. After he had finally dozed off, the friend saw his opportunity: he came near very silently, took hold of a branch that was poking out from under the fire, and ran off with it, leaving behind a trail of live, incendiary sparks.

Without realizing that the flame at the top of the burning branch continued to eat through the wood, the bearer was very shortly made aware of it the hard way. He suddenly let out a mighty scream, for the fire had scorched his wrist. But worse still, he let go of the blazing torch and ran home in utter agony. He had not gone very far when he heard a roaring sound behind him. Turning around, he saw a mighty conflagration following him, many times greater than the original cosy fire fed by the hunter. The soaring flames surrounded him threateningly. He screamed like someone demented, and fled away at a great speed.

As it darted along and spread over the savannah, the blaze devoured everything in its path: the grass, the shrubs, and even entire trees. It appeared to expand and then separate into several swelling streams of fire, each stream drifting listlessly with the wind across the savannah until it formed a massive curtain from horizon to horizon. The inferno took on nightmare proportions for it seemed as if the whole sky was going to catch fire and that the stars would shortly be ablaze. Even though the fire robber sped ahead faster and faster, the flames easily caught up with him. Completely surrounded by a ring of fire, he was thus rooted in one place and stricken with terror. However, as the fire charged along its reckless and destructive path, he discovered how he could avoid being burned to death. He noticed that it never scorched the same place twice: it would not go over a plot of grass or woodland that it had already consumed.

The fire continued to spread farther and farther until it finally came to a halt by a river. But it had left much destruction and desolation in its wake, including a number of villages. Fortunately the inhabitants saved their lives by wading into the river but they lost their dwellings, farms and gardens. Once the fire had burned itself out, the destitute people returned cautiously to face the devastation and to wonder at this mysterious misfortune. In the villages they soon discovered that all their food had been burned and as they were very hungry they began to eat what was left of it. A pleasant surprise awaited them, for the food that was not actually scorched to a cinder, tasted so much better than the raw meat that they had eaten formerly. They made another interesting discovery, too. Their clay pots, far from being destroyed by the flames, were now baked and much more durable. Ever since then people have been firing their pottery to give it greater endurance and beauty.

But what of the hunter and the original fire that he had so lovingly tended? What had happened to them? No sooner had the new fire begun its raging than the hunter woke up from his resting place beside his fire. He was horrified at the sight ahead of him. Meanwhile, the first fire burned on as before, gently consuming the logs that the hunter had provided for it. This fire began to speak: 'The destruction you see in front of you is the result of an attempted robbery. A man came and attempted to take me away. Now you can see what happens when a fire is removed from its stony resting place. Here I am docile, beyond I turn into a consuming monster that destroys everything in my path. But I can also help you to create useful things: I can bake your clay pots and in them you can cook your food; I can roast your prey; I can fire and forge metals. When treated with respect I can be the most valued friend of man.'

A Home for the Sun and the Moon

Chaga (Tanganyika)

In the beginning the sun and the water both dwelt on the earth and were inseparable friends. Very often the sun would visit the place where the water lived and they would keep company, talking together for many hours. But the water never visited the sun in his place, so the sun asked his friend one day, 'How is it that neither you nor your relations ever come to pay me a visit? My wife, the moon, and I would be very happy to offer you our hospitality.'

The water smiled and said, 'I do apologize for not having visited you until now,' he said, 'but the fact is that your house is far too small for me and for all my relations. I fear that we would probably drive you and your wife out of doors.'

'But we are about to build a new place,' replied the sun. 'Will you come and visit us if it is big enough?'

'It would have to be very large indeed for me to come in,' explained the water, 'for my people would take up so much space. What if we were to damage your belongings?'

These excuses saddened the sun and so to make him feel better, the water promised to visit his friend when his new property was ready, 'so long as it was really big.'

So the sun and his wife, the moon, started to work on a new home. With the help of many friends they built an enormous mansion.

'Surely now you can come and visit us,' pleaded the sun. 'For we are certain that our place is large enough to hold any number of visitors.'

But the water was far from convinced. Nevertheless, because the sun insisted, the water advanced towards the sun's new abode. Through the central door he flowed, bringing with him hundreds of fish, some water rats, and even a few water snakes. By now the water level was knee deep.

'Do you still want my people and me to enter further into your home?' he asked.

'Yes, of course,' cried the silly sun, 'bring them all, bring them all.'

So the water continued to flow into the new house until finally the sun and the moon were forced to climb onto the roof of their house to keep dry.

'Are you still certain that you want my people and me to come into your place?' repeated the water. Now the sun was too proud to go back on his word, so he replied, 'Yes, I just told you; I want everyone in. Tell them all to come.'

Finally the water rose to the very top of the roof, which forced the sun and the moon to go right up into the sky, where they have remained ever since.

The Fruit of Generosity

The Alur, who live on the shore of Lake Albert, believe in the power to talk to and get help from the natural forces, such as, in this story, Lightning.

Two boys lived in the same village. They were the same age and used to go out together to find things to do. One day they went into the bush and set snares to catch birds. The first boy was lucky – he caught a pigeon. But the second boy was unlucky – he caught only a spider. Out of pity for the spider, he let it go free.

The next day they went into the bush again to set snares. Once more the first boy was lucky – he caught a fat guinea-fowl, which makes a fine meal. But the second boy was unlucky – he caught only a stray bolt of lightning, which somehow became entangled in his snare. Seeing the lightning trapped and helpless he released it back into the sky, since it is impossible to eat lightning.

The following day, both boys were called before the king. He wanted them to cut him some new grinding stones. A grinding stone is a large flat stone used to grind cereals. To cut a grinding stone is a difficult job, usually done by professional stone-cutters, who hew the stone directly out of the rock. Wondering what they were going to do, the two boys went out to a rocky outcrop that stood near the village. There they tried their best to cut some stones, but all they succeeded in doing was to blunt their fathers' axes. They knew that the king would be angry if they failed in their task. In desperation the unlucky boy remembered the lightning he had released – maybe the lightning would help.

'Lightning!' he called, 'I freed you from my snare. Now I need your help. Please come and cut some grinding stones for me.'

Suddenly the lightning came. The sky flashed as bolts of lightning repeatedly struck the rock face. Sparks of fire flew and pieces of rock split off in all directions until a pile of perfectly shaped grinding stones lay on the ground before the boys. All the people in the village heard the thunder and saw the flashes of lightning. They came hurrying to see what had happened. When they saw the pile of grinding stones they were amazed, and helped the two boys to carry the stones to the king.

The king was very pleased with the boys, but now he wanted them to do something even more difficult. He asked them to bring him a star down from the sky. No one had ever done this before, and the boys had no idea how they could possibly do it. Then the unlucky boy remembered the spider he had released from his snare – maybe the spider would help.

'Spider! I freed you from my snare. Now I need your help. Please bring me a star from the sky.'

The spider heard his call for help. It spun an enormous web which reached from earth to sky. Then it climbed up into the sky and plucked a star which it dragged back down to earth. The boys brought the star to the king.

The king was very pleased with them, especially with the second boy, who had seemed unlucky, but who had then achieved such wonderful things for the king. The boy was rewarded with many cows and baskets of food. He became wealthy and popular. All because he had been generous enough to release the spider and lightning from his snares.

3
Gods and Spirits

Spirits of the Bush

This Yoruba story of Kigbo ('obstinate person') demonstrates the African fascination with the idea of a magical force which, once unleashed, cannot be stopped. Another example is the Ashanti story of Anansi and his magic sword which, after killing all the enemy, cannot be stopped and goes on to kill the soldiers on Anansi's side as well, and eventually Anansi himself. Some versions of this story have a tragic ending with Kigbo and his family killed.

There once lived a young man called Kigbo who had a reputation in his village for being obstinate. Whatever others would say he would always contradict them. If someone suggested, 'Tomorrow let's harvest the corn,' Kigbo would say, 'No, tomorrow we should dig up the yams.' Or if someone said, 'Tomorrow let's dig up the yams,' he would say, 'On the contrary, tomorrow we should harvest the corn.' When people wanted silence he would play drums, and when they wanted drums he would stay silent.

Kigbo married a young girl of the village called Dolapo. He built a house of his own and they had a child whom they named Ojo. When the season for preparing the fields came, Kigbo's father spoke to him.

'Come Kigbo, it's time you had your own field. Come with me outside the village and I'll help you clear some new ground.' But Kigbo was obstinate.

'The fields around the village are all too small, father. Let's go into the bush to clear some new land there instead.'

'No one farms in the bush, son. Men must have their fields near their homes and the bush is dangerous.'

'But I want to farm in the bush far away from my home. I'm not frightened of the bush, I like it.'

So Kigbo's father asked his mother to reason with the boy.

'Don't go to the bush, son, the bush spirits will make trouble for you,' she said.

'They won't trouble me. My name is Kigbo.'

Finally the village elder spoke to him.

'Our ancestors have taught us to avoid the bush spirits. Do not try to farm in the bush.'

But the obstinate Kigbo took no notice. He went home to his wife Dolapo, with Ojo in her arms, and told her to make everything ready.

'Tomorrow I will go into the bush.'

The next morning he made an early start, with his lunch bag and his bush knife. He walked far into the bush until he came to what he thought would be a suitable spot and set to work. He began to chop down the undergrowth and the brushwood. The sound of all his chopping disturbed the bush spirits, who immediately came out of the trees on all sides.

'Who is chopping down the bush?' they cried.

'It is I, Kigbo.'

'This land belongs to us, the bush spirits.'

'I don't care,' retorted Kigbo, and carried on chopping.

'This land is our land,' replied the bush spirits. 'Whatever you do we will do too.' So they joined him in chopping down the brush. There were hundreds of them and the job was soon done. Then Kigbo began to gather the brush together and burn it.

'This land is our land,' cried the bush spirits. 'Whatever you do we will do too.' So they joined him in gathering and burning the brush, and the job was soon done. The day ended and Kigbo returned to his village, feeling well satisfied.

'Now that you have come back please stay here and don't return to the bush,' pleaded his father and mother.

'I am happy in the bush,' replied Kigbo. 'The bush spirits help me and no one tells me what to do.'

The next morning he gathered a sack full of seeds and said goodbye to his wife and son.

'I am going to sow corn on my farm in the bush. I will stay there until the corn has ripened. You wait here and when it is ready for harvest I will come for you.' And he went off to find his farm in the bush. Soon he got there and began to sow his seeds. Again the bush spirits appeared.

'Who's there?' they cried.

'It is I, Kigbo, come to sow my corn.'

'This land is our land,' they cried. 'Whatever you do we will do too.' So they took the seeds from his sack and started to sow them everywhere. In no time the job was done, and Kigbo went to a nearby village where he had friends to wait for the corn to grow.

Back in his own village Dolapo waited with Ojo. She waited a long time and no message came from Kigbo. She started to worry that something may have happened to him in the bush. So she set off to find him with her son on her hip. At last she came to the farm. The corn was grown, but she saw no sign of Kigbo. The little boy Ojo began to cry because he was hungry.

'I want some corn,' he cried.

'It's not ripe yet,' she told him, but still he cried, 'I'm hungry.'

Although the corn was not yet ripe, to keep him quiet she broke off one stalk for him to chew on.

Immediately the bush spirits appeared.

'Who is breaking the corn?'

'It is I, Kigbo's wife.'

'This land is our land,' they cried. 'Whatever you do we will do too.' So they all began to break the corn stalks. In no time all the corn lay broken on the ground. Just then, Kigbo returned.

'The corn is ruined!' he shouted when he saw the devastation.

'It was the bush spirits,' said Dolapo, 'Ojo was hungry so I broke off one stalk, and then they broke all the rest.' And she slapped Ojo. The bush spirits appeared.

'What are you doing?' they demanded.

'I slapped the boy to punish him.'

'This land is our land,' they cried. 'Whatever you do we will do too.' And they all crowded round the boy and began to slap him.

'See what you have done now,' Kigbo shouted at his wife, and he began to slap her.

'What are you doing?' demanded the bush spirits.

'Slapping my wife because she has caused so much trouble,' replied Kigbo.

'This land is our land,' they cried. 'Whatever you do we will do too.' And they all began to slap Dolapo. Kigbo yelled at them to stop, but they took no notice. He could bear it no longer. In frustration he hit himself on the head.

'What are you doing?' demanded the bush spirits.

'All is lost, so I am hitting myself,' replied Kigbo.

'This land is our land,' they cried. 'Whatever you do we will do too.' And they all began to hit Kigbo about the head. Kigbo and Dolapo with Ojo ran for their lives all the way back to their village, leaving the farm behind. When he got back to the village Kigbo was ashamed.

'What happened?' asked his father, but Kigbo didn't want to talk about it. The next day his father suggested that they go together to the land near the village and clear a field for planting.

'Yes,' Kigbo agreed meekly, 'I will come with you father.'

The Rock Spirit and the Child

This Alur story includes one of their priests, whose arts include rain-making. The mother of the child must have been a witch, because only a witch would neglect her child in this way.

A dark outcrop of rock stood in the middle of a valley. The local people knew that a spirit lived in this rock and used to give it regular offerings. One day a woman came that way with her baby in a sling, carrying a basket of millet. She was tired and hungry, so she sat beneath the shade of the rock to eat her noon meal. She put down her basket on the rock, and her baby wrapped in cloth beside it. Although she knew about the spirit who lived in the rock she was not afraid. She ate her food without bothering to first make an offering to the spirit. This made the rock spirit angry.

When the woman had finished eating and was sufficiently rested she got up to continue her journey. She picked up her baby and then bent down to lift the basket of millet, but found she couldn't lift it – it was stuck fast to the rock. So she put down her baby and tried again to lift the basket. This time she picked it up easily. Then she bent to pick up her child, but found she couldn't – now the baby was stuck fast to the rock. She struggled for some time to lift both her baby and the millet, but found that she was unable to carry both of them – one would always remain stuck to the rock. She realized that she was going to have to choose between her baby and the basket of millet. In a fit of anger she chose the basket of millet, and left her baby on the rock, at the mercy of the hot sun. Then she left and returned home without her baby, saying her baby had been eaten by a jackal.

In the days after this, people passing that way heard the sound of a baby crying coming from the rock. They went up to find the baby, but could not see anything. But still they clearly heard the baby crying. News spread to the nearby village, where the baby's father lived. He heard about it and guessed that this must be his missing baby. He consulted a diviner.

'This is the voice of your child who is trapped inside the rock,' advised the diviner. 'Go to the rock and make an offering of food to the rock spirit. Gather other people from the village, put your offering on the rock and I will invoke the name of Jokichana, the spirit of the rock.'

So the people of the village accompanied the father and his mother to the rock with an offering of food. As they approached the rock they heard a tiny voice sing to them.

'Wuye, wuye, the spirit has taken me, the spirit has taken me, and I am starving.'

The father placed the pots of food on the rock and then the people began to dance and beat their drums. The diviner called on the name of Jokichana. As the dancing and drumming, and the chanting of the rock spirit's name increased in tempo, the rock began to tremble. Suddenly, it split open, revealing the child inside. Hastily the child's grandmother took the child in her arms and comforted it. Everyone was overjoyed and thanked the rock spirit.

'Praise the great god of the rock!' they sang. The mother of the child ran away and was never heard of again in those parts.

The Bird Spirit

This story, also from the Alur, shows how close the spirits of animal and human are in the bush.

A man who lived near Lake Albert wanted to invite his friends to a meal, so he went into the forest and set a snare to catch an animal so that he could serve them cooked meat. That night a bird was caught in his snare. The next morning he sent his eldest son to see if any animal had been trapped and to bring home whatever was there. The boy walked through the forest until he came to the place where his father had set the snare. From a distance he could see a strange and beautiful bird struggling inside the trap. As he approached he heard the bird singing with a sweet and clear voice:

> Little boy, little boy,
> Kiri kija kija ki
> What have you come to do?
> What have you come to see?

The bird's song captivated the boy, with its beautiful melody. He found himself answering in the same tune:

> Pretty bird, pretty bird
> Although you are so sweet
> I have come to capture you
> For my dad to eat!

The boy was astonished to find that he had sung such a song to the bird. He could not bring himself to take the bird home and see it cooked and eaten. So he ran back to tell his father.

'Daddy! Daddy! A very strange bird is caught in your snare in the forest which sang to me in our language. It asked me why I had come there, and then I sang back to it. I couldn't bring myself to take it home, so I left it there.'

'What nonsense is this?' said his father. 'Birds don't sing our language. You must have been imagining things. I will send your brother. He will bring back the bird so that it can be cooked and eaten.'

So the boy's brother went to the forest to bring back the bird. Again the same thing happened. As the boy approached, the bird sang to him in its lovely voice:

> Little boy, little boy,
> Kiri kija kija ki
> What have you come to do?
> What have you come to see?

The second boy was just as struck as his brother, and he too sang in reply:

> Pretty bird, pretty bird
> Although you are so sweet
> I have come to capture you
> For my dad to eat!

The boy could not bring himself to capture this beautiful creature, especially after he had sung to it. So he too ran home to his father.

'Daddy, it's true! The bird sings with a beautiful voice. It sang to me! I couldn't catch such a magical bird.'

'This is impossible!' shouted the father. 'I will have to go and see for myself about getting this bird. I am not going to be taken in by any such nonsense.' But when the father reached the spot where the bird was caught in his snare, again the bird sang to him:

> My son, my son,
> Kiri kija kija ki
> What have you come to do?
> What have you come to see?

The man was disturbed. What was this creature which called him 'my son' and sang with a human voice? Without wishing to, the father found himself singing in reply:

Gods and Spirits

> Pretty bird, pretty bird,
> What I've come to do
> Is catch you and kill you,
> And take you home and to stew!

Although he was surprised and couldn't understand what was happening, the man was determined to do as he had said. So he caught the bird and killed it. He took it home and gave it to his wife to cook. When he told his friends what had happened – how the bird had sung to his two sons and to him – they all decided that after it was cooked they should take it to the ancestor shrine outside the village. Here they regularly made offerings to their ancestors so that their spirits would be at peace. They took the flesh of the bird, cooked in a special dish, and offered it to their ancestors. Then, beginning with the elders, they prepared to eat it.

Just then an astonishing thing happened. Before their eyes the cooked bird on the dish lifted its head, opened its eyes, and sprang to life. Spreading its wings, now full of feathers again, it flew high up into the sky and was not seen again. After a moment's silence, everyone began to talk at once. What did it mean? Was it a good omen or bad? The father who caught the bird asked the elders of the village. At length they spoke.

'This bird was the spirit of your father. After he died he had to live as a bird in the forest. What has happened is good. His spirit has been released and is now free.'

The Origin of Night and Day

A Yoruba story, centred around a mysterious and frightening bush spirit, which explains the origins of night and day, why wild vines are so tangled, and why ants are always crawling up and down them.

In the beginning of time, when the earth was young, there was no day and night, only greyness over everything. In those times there lived a wealthy man whose name was Ojalugba. He kept many slaves who had to work hard for him all day. Among them was a boy called Ogungbemi. One day, feeling in an irritable mood, Ojalugba called Ogungbemi.

'I want you to go into the bush and collect a pile of wood as high as your head and carry it back to the village by nightfall.'

Poor Ogungbemi had no choice than to do as he was told. He went into the bush and spent a long time gathering together a big pile of wood. When it was as high as his head he tied it together into a bundle and tried to lift it onto his head. Try as he might he simply couldn't manage it. It was too heavy for him. Ogungbemi began to cry, because he knew that if he didn't come back to the village carrying the bundle Ojalugba would be angry with him and would give him some terrible punishment.

After he had been crying for some time, a strange and terrifying figure appeared from the bush. Ogungbemi fell silent and stood frozen to the spot, gripped with fear.

'My name is Fearsome,' the figure spoke with a voice like the cracking of trees.

Ogungbemi remained speechless with fright, his tongue and mouth dry.

'Your master has given you too much to carry. I will help you, but you must say nothing. If you tell them in the village about me then I will come and carry you away to the bush for ever.'

Ogungbemi knew that he faced severe punishment if he returned without the wood, so he had no choice other than to accept the offer of this fearful character. At last he spoke.

'Help me then, and I will say nothing to anyone.'

Fearsome strode forward and effortlessly lifted the bundle. He placed it on Ogungbemi's head, and amazingly Ogungbemi could hardly feel the weight of it. It seemed to him that it weighed no more than a small basket of cotton. With no difficulty he set off to walk back to his village. After some time he arrived home and easily put the bundle down beside Ojalugba's house. The people in the village saw the boy carrying the huge pile of wood and were surprised. They couldn't understand how such a small boy could carry such a heavy load. Some of them tried to lift it themselves but found it was impossible. Talk began to spread through the village.

'The boy must have had help from some bush spirit,' people said. But Ogungbemi refused to talk about it. He was frightened that Fearsome would come for him if he spoke the truth, so he thought it wiser to remain silent. Then Ojalugba heard about what had happened. He came out to see the bundle of wood and tried to lift it himself, but he couldn't. He turned to Ogungbemi and demanded to know who had helped him lift such a heavy load. The boy kept silent.

'Talk to me boy! I want slaves who answer me when I speak to them. I have so many slaves, one less will mean nothing to me. If you don't talk I'll have you beaten and thrown into the river.'

Now Ogungbemi was even more afraid of his master than he was of Fearsome. So at last he spoke.

'When I was in the bush I was frightened because I couldn't carry the bundle of wood. Then a bush spirit appeared. He said his name was Fearsome. He helped me to carry the bundle by making it light. But he told me that if I told anyone about him he would carry me away to the bush for ever.'

'This bush spirit will never be able to take you,' said Ojalugba, 'I shall see to it.' And he posted all his guards to protect the village. Armed with weapons they took their positions.

That night Fearsome crept out of the bush. He brought with him a magic powder. When he sprinkled it on the ground all the guards and the people of the village fell into a deep sleep. Then he picked up Ogungbemi and carried him off into the bush on his shoulders. But as Ogungbemi was being carried off he woke up and began to sing.

Saworo-jin-winni-jin-woro!
Why is this village asleep?
The cocks have stopped crowing,
The fires have stopped smoking,
The men have stopped hoeing,
The women have stopped cooking.
Ojalugba, Ojalugba, rescue me!
Saworo-jin-winni-jin-woro.

Ojalugba heard Ogungbemi's song. He got up and wakened all his guards and sent them off in pursuit of Fearsome. They followed him into the bush where they eventually caught up with him. There was a great struggle. Fearsome drew some more magic powder from a pouch at his waist and sprinkled it on the ground. At once everywhere became black, as dark as a deep cave. But the guards had their own magic powder. They threw some of it on the ground and everywhere became bright and light. Then Fearsome sprinkled some more of his powder on the ground and made it all dark again, then the guards sprinkled theirs and made it light. So they went, back and forth.

And they wrestled. Fearsome was very powerful, he wrestled with them all at once and they could not defeat him. They all remained locked in combat day after day, their bodies all tangled up together. As time passed, they turned into bush vines, such as grow up the bush trees, twisted and tangled up and down. The boy Ogungbemi, who was caught in the midst of them, became a swarm of ants crawling amongst the bush vines.

And so the struggle has continued to this day. Still you can see the bush vines with the swarms of ants crawling over them. The magic powders thrown on the ground by Fearsome and the village people create dark and light. The old greyness of the world is now changed forever to dark and light, night and day, in their perpetual rhythm of change.

The Underwater World

This enchanting story from the Alur, who live beside Lake Albert, shows their fascination with the lake and the mysteries it keeps.

When Anguza was still a young man he used to fish in the deep and mysterious waters of Lake Albert. One day he rowed his boat further from shore than he had ever been before. He had been told that the further out one went, the larger and more plentiful the fish became. As he rowed, the shoreline receded until all he could see in all directions was the silvery surface of the lake reflecting the blue sky. Still he rowed amid the great silence. Suddenly he noticed that the drops of water on his oars were glistening like pearls. He splashed the water and a spray of rainbow-coloured droplets flew through the air and tinkled back into the lake. Then he scooped some of the water into his boat. It fell before his eyes as shining pearls which rolled around the bottom of his boat.

Now he looked carefully at the water, and as he gazed into its depths, he saw what looked like large white fish swimming just below the surface. As he looked closer he saw that they were almost like goats – in fact they were goats: beautiful, creamy-coloured goats gliding through the water.

Mesmerized, Anguza jumped overboard into the water. He sank down, lower and lower. As he sank he saw all around him hundreds of goats. Eventually he reached the bottom. It was not slimy and grey, as you might expect – it was emerald green and rich with grasses. Everywhere were goats grazing on these luscious meadows of the deep. From among the goats appeared a human figure of unearthly beauty. He was the Lake God, Jokinam. Anguza sank to his knees in wonder before him. Jokinam embraced him and made him his goatherd. So Anguza looked after the white goats and stayed there on the bottom of the lake. He lived a wonderful life, just like a dream in paradise. He always had plenty of good food to eat and sweet milk to drink. In time he forgot all about his former earthly life as he wandered through the watery lands of the lake. In this way he passed time, and lost count of how many days, weeks or years went by.

One day memory returned to him. He remembered his wife and children, who must be waiting for him. Maybe they thought he was dead. He spoke to the Lake God.

'I want to go back home now.'

'You are free to go on one condition,' he replied. 'You must never tell anyone what you have seen down here. If you do you will die at once.'

So the Lake God returned him to the surface. There was his boat, still full of pearls. He found himself sitting in it again, and saw that the pearls were piled up around his feet. With an effort he began to row. After a long time he reached the shore again and found his way home back to his family. He was happy to be home, but he was different somehow. His family found him a changed man, given to silence. He hid the pearls in a cave and told no one what he had seen. Little by little he sold his pearls, and with the money he bought white cows. He no longer went fishing – instead he herded his cows and became a rich man.

One day he was invited to a party. There was a lot of beer and merry-making. He drank too much and forgot himself. Without thinking he began to talk aloud.

'I have been to the bottom of the lake. I have herded the Lake God's goats and drunk their milk...' Before he could say more he fell down, dead on the spot.

The people were afraid. They consulted the diviner to find out what had happened to Anguza.

'He gave away the secret of the lake,' it was Jokinam, the Lake God, speaking through him. 'Whoever gives away my secrets must die.'

The Country Under the Earth

Another mystical underworld tale from the Alur.

A young man once borrowed his brother's axe.

'Do not break it or lose it,' his brother warned. 'Or I shall be very angry.'

The man promised to be careful and set off to the forest to cut down a tree. He found a suitable tree and began to strike it with the axe. But the wood was so hard that it broke off the axe-blade, which fell into a hole in the ground at the base of the tree. He knelt down on the ground and peered into the hole. Inside it was dark and he could not see anything. He reached in but could feel no bottom. He stuck in his leg but still could feel nothing. He gradually lowered himself into the hole, but still was unable to reach the bottom. As he did so, he fell in.

The young man fell a long, long way until he found himself on a high road beneath the earth. Not knowing what to do, he decided to travel along it. Eventually he reached a town. In the centre of the town he found a noble palace, belonging to the king of that country. He went to the gate house where he was stopped by a guard. The king's minister was called to speak to him.

'Where do you come from and what do you want?' challenged the minister.

'I come from the country above, where I was cutting wood in the forest. My brother's axe-blade fell down into your world. I have come here to find it.'

'Wait here,' the man said and disappeared. After a while he returned. 'I have spoken to the king and he says he will see you in the morning. Now follow me.' And he led the young man to a guest house, where he was served an excellent meal and given a comfortable bed for the night.

The next day he was taken before the King Beneath The Earth, who was seated on a grand throne. The young man saw that the king's eyes sparkled like stars on a clear night, and that his gaze was piercing like fire. He was frightened, but the king ordered his servants to bring a seat to honour this guest from the country above.

'Do not fear,' the king told him, 'My people will find your brother's axe-blade and tomorrow they will take you back to your home.'

The people of the country beneath the earth searched for the axe-blade and found it. He passed another night with them, amid feasting and drinking. The following morning he was presented not only with the axe-blade, but also with a fine white cow and four well-fed goats.

'Now we will lead you back to your country. But you must be careful,' advised the minister. 'Do not tell anyone what you have seen down here. If you do you will die in an instant.'

The people led the young man back along the road. The road led to the mouth of a cave, where they said goodbye. He entered the cave alone, with his cow and four goats. Inside the cave was dark, but he saw in the distance a hole and through it the sky. He drove his animals through the hole and emerged into the sunlight, finding himself back beneath the tree in the forest. He hurried home and returned his brother's axe. He never told a soul what he had seen and lived peacefully ever after.

4
Animals and Humans

The Beautiful Hind

This moving story from Nigeria tells of the transformation of a hind into a woman. Such transformations are not uncommon in African folk-lore, and show how close together are the human and animal worlds.

There was once a handsome young man who lived with his wife in a village and earned his living as a hunter in the bush. They had a happy marriage and lived together peacefully. One day as the sun rose he left his village early in the morning to hunt. When he came to the bush he climbed a tree to hide and watch for game.

All day long he sat in the tree but no animals came his way. Just as the sun was setting a very graceful hind came running up to the spot just beneath the tree, not seeing the hunter hidden there. Carefully the young man fitted an arrow to his bow and prepared to shoot. But as he took aim he hesitated. The hind was behaving strangely. It appeared to be hiding amongst the bushes and struggling with something. To his astonishment, the hunter saw that the hind was shedding its skin. As he watched, fascinated, he saw a beautiful young girl emerge from the skin. She took the skin and carefully rolled it into a bundle which she hid under a stone in the bushes. She did this with such grace and her beauty was so striking that the young man could only gaze awestruck at her. He had never seen a woman so beautiful. She stood up, shook herself nervously and looked this way and that. Still not seeing him she ran off in the direction of the next village.

As soon as she was gone the young man jumped down from his tree and searched for the skin which she had hidden in the bushes. Finding it he held it up in the dying rays of the sun to admire its beauty. But even more, he remembered the beauty of the young girl he had just seen. Somehow he must see her again. So as night fell he put the skin in his bag and walked home through the bush. By the time he got home it was dark and his wife was waiting for him.

'Why are you late my love?' she asked. 'And what is in your bag?'

'I waited all day for an animal to kill, but nothing came, so my bag is empty.' He didn't tell her about the strange hind, and he carefully hid the skin under the floor of his hut.

That night he could hardly sleep. All he could think about was the strange beauty he had seen in the bush. The next morning he set off back to the same place to see if he could catch another glimpse of her. He climbed the same tree and hid. All day long he waited without seeing her, and the more he waited the more lovesick he became. Then, just as the sun was setting, he saw her come at last. He watched as the beautiful girl searched among the bushes for her skin. She became confused. She hurried this way and that from bush to bush and from stone to stone. Feverishly she scratched the ground and began to wail.

'Where has it gone? My precious skin – who has taken it? I must find it before nightfall – without it I cannot live.'

'I can help you,' called the young man from the tree.

Startled, she looked to see where the voice was coming from. At last she saw him in the tree.

'Who are you,' she said in fear. 'And what do you want?'

'Yesterday I saw you take off your skin and after you had gone I took it home with me,' he said. 'Now I have fallen in love with you. If you agree to come with me and be my wife I will return your skin.' He felt sorry for her but he was completely captivated by her beauty, and knew he must have her for his own.

She was trapped. Desperately she tried to reason with him. If he would return her skin she would give him anything, but not marry him. But he was determined to have her. At last she was forced to give in to him, but she made him promise secrecy.

'Not everything seen by eye should be told by mouth. Promise not to tell any human what you have seen today.' And sadly she followed him to his home. At nightfall he entered his home with the girl. His wife was surprised to see her and asked who she was.

'I met her in the next village,' he lied, 'and the king of the village insisted I marry her. He said her previous husband had died and no one else would look after her. So I agreed to take her in. Other men in the village have two wives. Why shouldn't I? Please be kind to her and treat her as your younger sister.'

His first wife was angry and upset, but she had no choice than to accept this new co-wife. She resented her for her beauty and was deeply suspicious of her. Who was this girl who threatened to disrupt her home which had been so happy? She resolved to bide her time.

Time passed. The new wife seemed to settle in. At first everyone in the village was distrustful of her. She seemed so unusual and strange in her ways. She didn't know how to cook or clean or how to sing the village songs like other girls. But she was beautiful with her dark eyes and her animal-like energy and they were all fascinated by her. Gradually she came to be accepted.

And the young man had eyes only for her. At first she would beg him to return her skin. But he refused – he didn't want to lose her. Gradually she began to forget about her past and to accept her new life. Although he had been cruel to her she had nowhere else to go. She depended on him, and clung to him as if he were the only person in the world. He was the only one who really understood her, who knew the truth about who she really was. He spent all his time with her and forgot his first wife. He didn't care that the girl couldn't cook or look after the home. The elder wife, who still had to do most of the work, grew more and more jealous.

Reluctantly she taught the girl how to cook and help with the household duties, but she was clumsy round the house. She didn't fit in, with her curious dark eyes and her animal ways. The first wife knew that her husband hadn't told the truth about this girl, and she wanted to know what he was hiding, so she determined to find out who this strange girl was who had so upset her life. She went to the Babalawo, the village priest, for help, and he gave her a powder, saying, 'Give your husband a good meal with plenty of palm wine, then dissolve this powder in his third calabash of wine and ask him to tell you about her.'

That evening she cooked a lavish feast for her husband, with plenty of palm wine. The hunter enjoyed eating and drinking, suspecting nothing. While the young wife was away at the well washing the pots, the older wife dissolved the powder into his third calabash. When he had drunk it he felt a little strange. His wife asked him to tell her more about the girl. He began to talk. It was as if he had lost all self-control. He found he was saying too much, but he couldn't stop himself. Within a few minutes he had told her the whole story, even where he had hidden the skin. Then he fell into a drunken sleep.

The girl returned from the well carrying the pots. Seeing the hunter sleeping she quietly entered the hut. Suddenly the elder wife confronted her. 'What's this?' she demanded, throwing the skin at her.

'I – I don't know,' exclaimed the girl, caught by surprise.

'Take it, you animal, and go back to the bush where you belong,' screamed the older woman with a voice full of hatred. 'Leave here and never come back!'

The girl recognized the skin. She remembered her past life and the cruel way she had been imprisoned. Her anger and frustration burst forth. She took her skin and in an instant had put it on. The hind leapt up, its hooves flashing in the face of the elder woman, striking her again and again. Mortally wounded, the woman fell to the ground, and the hind raced off into the night.

In the morning the young man awoke from his drunken sleep. As he opened his eyes he called out for his beloved, but there was no answer. He searched everywhere for her, but somehow he didn't notice his wife's body lying in the corner. Then he saw that the skin was missing from its hiding place. In a panic he ran into the bush shouting for his sweetheart. All day long he searched for her. At nightfall he returned home, his head hung low. Still he didn't know that his elder wife was harmed.

When he returned, tired and despondent, he saw in the corner of the hut his dead wife, ugly wounds on her face and head. In shock he wept all night. Next morning he went out into the village for help. The people came and saw what had happened. They buried his wife. He never saw the beautiful young girl again, or the hind. His whole life had turned to ashes. He lived for many years alone, haunted by the memory of his happy marriage, and his fateful meeting with the beauty of the bush. Unable to forget the past he died a sad and lonely death.

The Hunter's Secret

Another shape-changing story of Nigeria, this time demonstrating the importance of keeping such magical things secret.

There was once a small village in which lived a hunter whose skill was legendary. Everyone had heard stories of how he had miraculously escaped the charges of enraged elephants and the pounce of tigers. But it was not all down to his bravery for he had some magic powers to help him. He could change his shape to many different types of living things if he was in danger.

After many years of seeing their brothers and sisters being killed by this hunter the animals finally came to know about his powers. Because the elephants were the ones who were worst affected, one of them was chosen to try and find out the hunter's secret. One particular elephant had the power to change his skin to that of a man at will, and so he was selected for the task.

When the hunter came home the next day, he found a stranger waiting for him. He found out that the stranger was also a hunter and welcomed him into his house and invited him to stay the night. They ate well and drank much. The hunter was becoming more and more talkative from the palm wine and soon the stranger (who was really the elephant in the form of a man) thought that it was the right time to ask him about his secret.

'I have heard about your great escapes from charging elephants,' he said, 'how do you do it?'

'It is very simple,' replied the hunter. 'I know some magic words and when I recite them I can change my shape into that of grass.'

'But what do you do if the animal walks on and rips up the grass?'

'The grass is only the beginning. After that I can change into a tree.'

'Yes, but what if the animal knocks down the tree?'

The hunter went on telling the elephant-man all the different things he could change into. 'But,' he continued, 'there comes a time when I can change no longer. When I become that final thing I am vulnerable and if attacked, I would surely die. That final thing is...'

But before he could say another word the hunter's wife, who had been listening to the whole conversation, interrupted him. 'My dear husband, you are being very foolish. You are telling your most important secret to a stranger. Have you lost your mind? A wise man does not tell everything he knows to anyone, not even his wife.'

The hunter suddenly realized what he was about to do and, much to the disappointment of his guest, he stopped himself. He was relieved. But he had already told the stranger too much. Still it could not be helped now. 'My friend,' said the hunter, 'I am getting tired. Let us sleep now.' And so they slept. The next day the elephant returned to his original form and went back to the bush.

The hunter continued with his hunting and nothing strange happened for several days. Then one day he happened upon a very large elephant. He was just preparing to fire an arrow when the creature turned towards him and charged. The surprised hunter quickly spoke the words and changed to a blade of grass.

But the elephant, who was the very same one who had stayed at the house of the hunter, went straight for the grass and started to trample it. The frightened man changed into a tree but the elephant again lost no time in trying to uproot the tree. Each time the man changed into something else the elephant knew what it was and tried to destroy him.

Finally the hunter changed himself into his final form, a tiny water insect on the lake. The elephant did not know what to look for. In a rage he destroyed everything around. After thrashing around for quite a long time, the elephant finally tired himself out and retreated. He had to go back and tell all the other creatures that he had failed and the hunter was still very much alive.

The tiny insect that was the hunter changed back through all the various forms up to the blade of grass and finally back into the man. Then he calmly collected his bow and arrow, and returned home to thank his wife who had saved his life.

The Leopard and the Boy

(Source unknown)
A touching story of friendship between boy and animal. But although the human and animal worlds may mingle, they will always remain apart.

There once lived a very rich man who had many wives. One day he found out that a nearby tribe was about to attack his village. Afraid for himself and his family, he decided that they would all leave the village that night. And so they packed their most precious possessions and left. But it just so happened that one of the wives was just about to give birth and she was therefore very slow.

'You must go faster my dear,' urged the husband. 'If we go this slow, we will be caught by the tribe.'

But she just could not go any faster and now the man faced a very hard decision. If he left his wife behind alone, she would surely be killed by wild beasts but if he and all the others waited for her they would all be captured. So he set off with all his other wives and children, leaving his pregnant wife to die.

The next morning the woman gave birth to a baby boy. The frightened mother took her baby and went deep into the forest to try and find a place which was safe from both the enemy tribe and from wild animals. Finally she found such a place and there she built a shelter. She stayed there for many years, only leaving the place to get food. The boy grew up with his mother and played with the young animals that he met in the forest.

One day he met a leopard cub. They played together and formed a good friendship and they both agreed to meet regularly. After a time, they found out they were both the same age and neither of them had a father. They spent more and more time together, but the boy was frightened that his mother might be killed by the leopard's mother. The cub assured the boy that his mother would not have to leave her place of safety because he would bring meat to them every day.

One day, however, the boy's mother went out in search of water and was killed by the leopard. When the cub saw the body he was very sad. He set out to find the boy and break the bad news to him. As could be expected the boy was full of grief, but the cub reassured him by promising to look after the orphan and always to make sure he had enough food. They both went to the leopard's cave and became such good friends that they were like brothers.

One day the leopard noticed that the boy was very sad so he asked what was troubling him.

'My dear friend,' he told the leopard, 'my mother told me that if you want to have a happy life then it is necessary to make a sacrifice to the gods. But to make a sacrifice I need snails, kola nuts and palm nuts. The only place to get these things is in the market but I have no money. What shall I do?'

'Do not be upset,' the leopard replied, 'for I will go to the market myself and get you the things you need.'

So on the next morning before anyone was up the leopard went to the market and climbed up a tree. By the middle of the day the market was full of people and he jumped down into the middle of them. Everyone was very scared. They all ran for their lives, leaving the market empty. The leopard then went round the stalls taking what the boy needed. When he returned the boy thanked the leopard and made his sacrifice.

A couple of months later, the leopard noticed that the boy had become sad again. When he asked what the matter was the boy replied that he wanted some clothes. Although the leopard did not think that the boy actually needed any clothes, he still agreed to try and get some for him at the market. The next day he repeated the same plan as before and got clothes for the boy.

After another few months had passed the boy again became sad. When the leopard asked him what was troubling him this time, he replied, 'All men my age get married. I also want to get married but how can I?'

'I am your friend,' replied the leopard, 'why do you want someone else? Am I not good enough for you?'

'Of course. You are the best friend I could ever have wished for but I still need a wife. Don't worry, if I get a wife it will not change anything between you and me. We will still be best friends.' After hearing this the leopard agreed to help the boy.

The next day they both went to market together. The leopard was dressed in some of the boy's clothes so that he would not scare anyone. As they were looking through the stalls the boy saw a very beautiful girl. He pointed her out to his companion and said he wanted her for his wife. The leopard assured the boy he would do his best to get her. It turned out that this girl was the daughter of the king which meant it would be very hard for the leopard to make her marry his friend. But he had come up with a plan already.

'Listen to me. Tomorrow I will go to the market and kill the princess. Then I will stay next to the body and no matter who tries to get the body I will not let them. They will want the body to bury her but I will not let them get near her. Then you will approach the body and I will not stop you. When you are over her you should squeeze some magic juice from this leaf into the girl's eyes and she will come back to life. After this the king will definitely let you marry her.'

So the next day the leopard killed the princess and stayed over the body. The king sent his best men to try and retrieve the body for burial but they were all so terrified of the leopard that none of them succeeded. Then the boy went up to the king and said that he would not only get the body away from the leopard but he would also return life to the princess. The king was doubtful but told the boy to have a go. He also told him that if he succeeded, he could marry her.

Everyone watched as the boy walked straight to the body and they all gasped as the leopard turned and ran back into the forest. The boy then bent down and picked up the princess. He carried her back to the king and laid her down. Word had spread around the town that the boy was trying to bring the king's daughter back to life, and everyone had come to watch. In front of them all, the boy took the leaf out of his pocket and squeezed its juice into the girl's eyes. Immediately she sat up and looked around puzzled. She asked her father what was going on because she couldn't remember anything that had happened.

The king was overjoyed and before long the boy and the princess were married. The king had a house built specially for the couple and they lived together happily.

The gardens of this new house extended all the way up to the edge of the forest. One night the boy sneaked into the forest to see his friend the leopard again. They talked about all that had happened and the boy told his friend to visit him every night in the gardens. The leopard was very happy that they could still be friends despite the boy's marriage and visited him every night.

Once, the boy's wife woke up in the middle of the night and could not find her husband. She looked for him everywhere and finally saw him at the bottom of the garden talking to a leopard. She was very frightened and was about to scream for help when the boy stopped her. He reassured her that this leopard was a friend and was harmless. He convinced her and she kept quiet.

But as time went on the girl became uneasy about the visits of the leopard. Finally she could take it no longer. She went to her father and told him about the nightly visits. He guessed this leopard was the same one that killed his daughter before. So he sent some of his guards to the garden to wait for the leopard.

That very same night when the leopard came out of the forest, he was attacked by a dozen guards. After being very badly wounded, he managed to escape to the forest. There he lay down and died. The guards returned to the palace and reported to the king that they had done their job.

When the boy went to the normal meeting place the leopard was not there. His fears were confirmed when he saw a trail of blood leading into the forest. He followed it until he came to the dead body of the leopard. Full of grief, he started to cry. Then, seeing that Tortoise was nearby, he begged him to get a magic leaf to bring the dead animal back to life. After much persuasion, Tortoise agreed and soon the boy squeezed the juice into the eyes of the leopard.

When he awoke the leopard was angry. He blamed the boy for what had happened.

'Do not be angry at me,' defended the boy, 'for I did not attack you. I don't even know why you were attacked or who by.'

Here Tortoise interrupted, 'It is no use blaming anyone for this. Two beings like yourselves are not meant to be friends. Neither in the animal kingdom, nor in the world of humans is it proper for you to be together. You should go your separate ways now.' Having said this, Tortoise took the branch of a palm tree and tore it apart. This was a symbol of separation and so the two friends separated, never to speak to each other again. And from that day onwards, humans and animals have never been friends.

Mokele

A Ntomba myth (Zaire)

The first man in the new creation was named Wai. He lived and ruled as the chief of a large village called Ntomba near Lake Tumba in Zaire together with his wives and slaves. One day he decided to set out from his home in order to embark upon a long hunting mission in the jungle. As he was about to leave, he bade farewell to his favourite wife, Moluka, who was soon to have a baby, saying, 'When I return from the hunt, I want to see my son already born and thriving.' Then he departed. Days and weeks went by, but Moluka's belly got no bigger, something which saddened her a great deal. And every day when she went down to the river to fetch water, she expressed her sorrow through a melancholy air that she improvized while she lowered and raised her clay water jug. Its words went like this:

Mother, O mother, tell me true;
When I shall see my baby new.

One evening, as Moluka was sitting and musing by the river's edge, she heard a crackling sound behind her, as if someone were walking on dry leaves and twigs. Looking around, she spotted what seemed to be an elderly lady coming out from behind the bushes.

'Have no fear, Moluka, wife of Wai, for I have come here in response to your plaintive song,' said the lady reassuringly. And with these words, she placed her right palm on Moluka's belly. All of a sudden an egg popped out.

'Behold,' cried the lady, 'this is what you have been carrying. Let me take it for the moment for only I know how to look after it. But do not neglect to come back here tomorrow morning with food for me to eat.' And then, in a flash, the elderly lady vanished into the night and Moluka, greatly shaken, returned to her home with her pitcher of water.

Early the next morning the young mother anxiously rushed back to the river's edge bearing a platter of the finest food. There waiting for her was the elderly woman, and in her rocking embrace was the most beautiful baby boy anyone had ever seen. The lady consumed all of the food that Moluka brought for her, while the happy mother held her child close and nursed him. When the lady had finished she said, 'Now I must take the child away once again, but make certain that you return tomorrow morning with more food.'

She seized the infant from Moluka's arms and disappeared with him as before, leaving the distraught mother alone and weeping. But very early the next morning she was back at the edge of the river with yet another sumptuous meal. The elderly lady came into sight once again but this time there was a little boy walking beside her.

'This is your son, Moluka. Look how quickly he has grown. Now you may take him home for I know that your husband will be returning shortly from his expedition. Only remember one thing: do not reveal your child to any other person today. Simply keep him inside your hut until he is fully grown.

That evening Wai came back to his home from the long hunt and in the morning all of the women in the village came out from their huts with their children in order to welcome him. All the women, that is, except Moluka, who timidly stepped out all by herself. Without exception, the other women mocked and scorned her when she appeared at the grand reception without a child.

'Ha! You Moluka were proud to be the chief's favourite wife, but see, you have not yet been able to bear him a baby!' they cried disdainfully. Chief Wai also could not hide his disappointment with Moluka. He also felt somewhat dishonoured because a tribal chief naturally expects all of his wives to bear him many children.

Wai thought about dismissing Moluka from his household when a disturbance was heard from Moluka's hut. It was a young man's voice which called out the following command: 'Door, be you open.' An unseen force opened the door of the hut and through the space appeared a tall, handsome youth. For several moments he stood in the doorway looking at the ground in front of him; then he issued another order: 'Remove yourself, O grass! How do you expect me to draw near to my father and to salute him?'

In an instant unseen hands cleared a path from the hut to where the chief was standing. Now the young man spoke sternly to the woven reed mats that were stacked in a pile beside Moluka's bed: 'Unroll yourselves this instant!' Apparently self-propelled, the woven reed mats flew through the doorway, unrolled themselves and lay flat in a neat row on the newly cleared path. After this the young man marched over the mats towards the place where the astonished Chief Wai was seated, surrounded by his many wives, all of them equally aghast.

'My humblest respects to you, O father and chief,' said the newcomer bowing low.

Animals and Humans

'Who are you?' asked Wai.

'I am your son, Mokele, child of Moluka,' came the reply. Chief Wai felt immense satisfaction at having this brave young lad as his new son and to reward Moluka, he decided to make her his most honoured spouse, much to the envy of the other wives.

Now these were the days before the sun had been charged to spread its rays over the earth. Thus, instead of sunshine, there was only moonshine; and oddly enough, the people of Ntomba called the moon the sun! One day Mokele asked his father, 'Can it be that the real sun does not rise each morning on Ntomba?'

'We do not understand what you mean,' replied Chief Wai. 'What is the sun?'

'I shall go and purchase it for you,' cried Mokele. He immediately began to dig out a large canoe from an old fallen tree and when it was finished, all of the wild animals from the forest came close to admire it. The wasps were the first to praise the workmanship.

'What a magnificent canoe,' they said as they buzzed around Mokele's head. And whispering in his ear, they added, 'We very much want to go with you on your mission to find the sun. For if its owners refuse to let you have it, we shall sting them!'

'Bokendela,' exclaimed Mokele to the excited wasps, which is to say, 'Come on board.'

The next visitor was Nkulu, the tortoise, who also requested permission to join Mokele on his journey to the land of the sun.

'How can you help me?' remarked the young man. 'Look how slow you are!'

'Slow indeed!' responded the tortoise embittered. 'Of all the wingless beasts am I not the first here? And what is more, I am the magician of combat; I shall be your war wizard. I can even discern the location of the sun though it be concealed from your sight.'

'Splendid!' cried out Mokele. 'Bokendela!' Shortly afterwards appeared Nkombe, the kite.

'May I journey with you, too?' asked the bird.

'How can we profit from your presence, kite Nkombe?'

'My contribution will be indispensable,' was the reply. 'For if they refuse to give you the sun, I shall simply pick it up and fly away with it.'

'Excellent! Bokendela! Come on board! Welcome!'

One by one, all the animals of the forest, following a similar procedure, managed to get a place in the canoe. Each managed to convince Mokele that its particular talent was invaluable for the successful completion of the expedition. Of course the canoe was now quite full but it nevertheless managed to cast off and travel easily eastward towards the land of the sun. Nkulu, the tortoise, took up a position in the prow of the vessel in order to maintain an accurate orientation while Nkombe, the kite, flew above keeping vigil and using his keen eyesight to spot any danger ahead.

After many weeks of travel through the waterways of the dense tropical rainforest, they arrived in the kingdom of the famous monarch Mokulaka. It was he who had possession of the sun. Mokele paid his respects to the venerable patriarch, and then asked respectfully, 'King Mokulaka, can I purchase the sun from you?' The king was most unwilling to part with the sun but did not say as much to his visitors from Ntomba. For he was quick to notice that in Mokele's entourage were the powerful leopard, the valiant baboon, and all the other animals of the forest.

'Even if I refuse to sell them the sun,' thought Mokulaka, 'what is to prevent them from taking it by force? What I must do is to delay the negotiations for as long as possible until I can get some reinforcements.' Then turning to the group he said, 'Very well, I shall be happy to sell the sun to you, but I request that you wait for my son, Yakalaki, before you take it so that we can all agree on a fair payment.'

Mokele could not see anything wrong with this request so he agreed and went away to rest. Meanwhile, the cunning ruler called at once for his daughter, the princess Molumbu.

'My dearest Molumbu,' said Mokulaka, 'you must help me get rid of this rabble. Go and prepare a strong poison which will kill these strangers.' Now as he was speaking these words, neither of them was aware that one of the wasps that had travelled with Mokele was well within hearing distance. Having overheard Mokulaka's evil plot, the wasp went swiftly back to his master in order to repeat what had been conspired.

Mokele realized that it was impossible to have any trust in the old king, so he decided to carry off the sun by force. Naturally, he pretended not to know anything about the ploy and thus went gladly with Molumbu into her hut. Now Mokele was an extremely good-looking young man and Molumbu could not resist admiring him. After they had spoken for a while, she decided that she could not obey her father's wishes, so she threw the jar of poison onto the floor and sent word to Mokulaka that she had gone to the woods to gather some fresh herbs.

In the meantime, the other animals were intensely preoccupied. True to his word, the tortoise divined that the sun was concealed in a cave, so he went to locate it, taking the kite with him. The tortoise lifted the sun out of its hiding place and in its claws, the kite clutched both the tortoise and the sun and soared with his load up high into the sky. This is how the sun rose for the first time.

As the sun's rays penetrated the forest, Mokele, Molumbu and the entire crew of animals sped to the canoe in order to make their escape. At that moment, Prince Yakalaki, Mokulaka's son, had returned to his father's kingdom, so he and his fighters gave chase, but the swarm of wasps descended on them like a cloud, stinging them so savagely that they beat a hasty retreat.

Mokele and his comrades experienced many exciting adventures on their way back to Ntomba through the waterways of the rain forest, but finally he arrived home with his new bride. His father, Wai, and all the people of Ntomba welcomed him as a champion and hero. He was attributed to have fixed the point of the rising sun 'up-river', which for the Ntomba people means 'east', since all rivers in that area of Central Zaire flow from east to west.

Chichinguane and Chipfalamfula

(*Mozambique*)

Makenyi was the chief of an important tribe in southern Mozambique. Like other village chiefs in that region, he had a great number of wives; but his newest and most favoured spouse had given him two very beautiful daughters. These two girls, in particular the older, whose name was Chichinguane, were Chief Makenyi's special pets. And as such they were the envy of the other wives and their children, all of whom were forever distant and hostile towards them.

One summer's day the girls from the village were sent by Makenyi to dig for clay to plaster the walls of their dwellings. The best clay was to be found in pits by the river bank, so that is where they headed. Upon their arrival, the most senior of all the girls instructed Chichinguane to climb down into the deepest pit and dig out clay for her. It was extremely dank and marshy down there and poor Chichinguane was forced to work standing in a swamp. She passed clay up to the other girl who filled her basket and then set off for her home in the village without caring to help pull Chichinguane out of the clay pit – even though she knew that the young girl could not climb out by herself.

Chichinguane looked around her in the deep pit. She was encircled by high walls of slippery clay except on one side where the deep river flowed by. To her alarm, the water level of the river was rising rapidly as a result of the heavy rain storms of recent weeks, and now it was up to her chest. It was only a matter of time and she would be completely covered by the water. Looking desperately for a means of escape, Chichinguane was horrified to see a huge, gaping mouth under the surface of the water. This mouth belonged to an enormous fish called Chipfalamfula, meaning

'Sealer of Rivers', which was so notorious that even Chichinguane had often heard tales about its fearsome adventures.

'Come into me, my child,' said the immense fish. 'Enter into my belly. When you live with me you will realize that there is no better place in the world to be.' Very cautiously, Chichinguane stepped into the mouth of the waiting sea monster and took her place inside its vast belly. It seemed to be as boundless as the heavens. Looking around her she was amazed to discover a large human population also in residence. In particular, many people were working in fields, cultivating and growing crops. There seemed to be an unlimited supply of food. Chichinguane remained inside the belly of the fish for many days, never in want of anything.

Weeks passed and one day the girls of Makenyi's village came down to the river bank, this time to draw water. On their heads and shoulders the children carried their water pots and as they walked towards the flowing river they sang songs and played games. Each one in her turn bent down to fill the pots in the water, then raised them effortlessly back onto their heads and shoulders. Only Chichinguane's little sister was unable to balance the weight of the full pot because she was so small and it was very heavy.

'How shall I manage?' cried the distraught little girl. 'Every time I try to lift the pot onto my head, I can not raise it higher than my knees! What else can I do?' She certainly had good reason to cry because it was impossible to convey the pot in any other way and her mother would reproach her vehemently if she were to come home with only half the amount of water needed. The other girls, being older and bigger, had already set off. They could balance their jugs high on their bodies without any problem. But all this young lady could do was sit down beside her full but unmovable pitcher and shed bitter tears.

As she stared into the flowing river the girl was most surprised to see her sister Chichinguane coming out of the rapids. Everyone had imagined that she had been drowned or carried away by the swirl. They embraced each other at once and Chichinguane helped her little sister to her feet, caressed and dried her tear-stained cheeks. Then she lifted the full pitcher of water onto the young girl's head and walked together with her to the village. But just before the first dwellings came into sight Chichinguane bade her sister farewell, went back to the river into which she plunged, and returned to her beloved Chipfalamfula waiting below.

The very same events took place the next day. All of the village girls came back to the river and again left the young sister in despair, unable to lift her full jug, and weeping sadly. Once more Chichinguane came to the rescue: she lifted the water pot for her and conducted her back to the village precincts. This happened day after day.

One evening the chief's favourite wife wanted to send her little daughter to him with a tasty brew that she had prepared. But the jug was far too heavy for the child to carry even though she made several valiant attempts to lift it. Observing this, the mother began to get curious.

'How is it that you bring me water every day from the river?' she asked.

'I get help,' the young child replied, 'Chichinguane turns up and lifts the pitcher onto my head. She also accompanies me back to the village because I am left totally alone by my step-sisters.'

The mother listened to her daughter's words in total disbelief. So the next afternoon she went with her little daughter to the river and lay in wait, concealed behind some shrubs. Eventually Chichinguane emerged from the river and, as before, assisted her little sister in balancing the water pot on her head. As soon as she saw her lost daughter, the mother came running out and attempted to embrace her.

'No, mother, stop!' exclaimed Chichinguane, 'Please do not try to hold me for now I am as one of the fish and my home is in the deep waters of the river.' And no matter how tightly her mother wrapped her arms around her, Chichinguane slid out of the embrace like a slippery eel and finally she vanished under the surface of the water where she now belonged.

Chichinguane returned to the safety of the Chipfalamfula's belly where she continued to live a peaceful and happy life. At times, however, she began to think wistfully of her home and family. She even spoke to the great fish about her mother, father and sister and confessed that she longed to be with them again in the village. After much thought the fish consented to her leaving and as a farewell present he gave her a magic wand.

In due course, Chichinguane stepped through the doorway of her mother's hut. At the time, she was clothed in an oily, scale-like fish skin but as she approached her mother she touched her skin with the wand saying, 'This fish's skin I bequeath to you.' All at once the shining scales fell off one by one and as they touched the floor of the hut, they turned into bright silver coins. With this small fortune that lay at her feet, the mother invited the entire village to a grand feast to celebrate her daughter's return to her home.

The other village girls were greatly incensed at these events: their envy knew no bounds. So they gathered together in secret to devise a new strategy to get rid of Makenyi's two daughters. Their opportunity came when the village chief sent all of them out to the forest to collect firewood. The eldest amongst them, the same girl who had abandoned Chichinguane in the clay pit, instructed the two sisters to climb up a tall tree, cut off its uppermost branches, and throw them down to the ground for collection. When she and the other girls had taken as much as they could carry, they ran off, leaving the two in the tree to make their own way down unaided. Just as the sisters were descending with the greatest caution, feeling their way down the trunk for firm footholds, a company of ogres turned up at the foot of the tree.

Now these ogres had the bodies of humans but only one leg each; they forever squabbled among themselves. But when they looked up and saw the two girls, they ceased their arguing immediately and began to hew vigorously at the trunk of the tree with an axe. Thankfully, Chichinguane was carrying her magic wand with her and whenever the tree began to teeter and lean, as if about to fall, she touched it with the charmed rod and the injury made by the ogres' axe healed in an instant. In this way the tree always stood erect and strong.

Seeing that they were getting nowhere, the ogres decided to take a break from their strenuous task in order to regain their energy. They lay down on the grass and very soon were fast asleep. Chichinguane chose not to delay any longer, she nudged her sister off the branch and leaped down beside her. The two of them landed with an extremely loud thud, so loud in fact that it startled the sleeping ogres and roused them into action again. Each one sprang up on his leg and began hopping furiously after the girls at a great speed.

The two girls sped ahead as fast as they could go but they could always hear the thumping of the ogres behind them as well as their shouts of abuse. Finally they came to the river bank and Chichinguane immediately dipped her magic wand into the flowing water, saying, 'Chipfalamfula, seal the river!' And in a twinkling the river stopped its flow and the two girls passed over dry shod on the river bed. As soon as they were safely on the other bank, Chichinguane stooped down and stroked the sandy ground with her wand, calling out, 'Chipfalamfula, release the waters!'

Meanwhile, the ogres had continued chasing the girls on the dry river bed. They were half way across when a great wave gushed over and engulfed them. Without any warning they were all swept away and drowned.

It was a lucky escape, but the girls still had far to go before they would reach their village. Night was falling and they had to walk back through a dense forest. On their way they noticed a large cave in the side of a hill and upon investigating it, they realized that they had come across the lair of the accursed ogres. To their immense surprise they discovered a hoard of stolen treasure: necklaces, pearls, corals, beads and gems. What is more, they also found the remains of the ill-fated souls that the ogres had taken and killed. Terrified by this ghoulish scene, the girls hastened out of the cave. But before they left, they decided to take with them as much of the treasure as they could carry and wear. It was now pitch black outside and they were at a loss to locate the forest path. Chichinguane then held her wand high above her head and ordered it to illumine their passage through the trees. Its top end shone like a blazing torch, lighting up the path that they assumed would take them close to their home.

When the sisters finally reached the forest's edge, the morning sunrays spanned over an open countryside. The territory resembled nothing they had ever seen before; they were completely lost. Ahead of them rose a strange and stately palace which was enclosed by a high wooden fence. At its gates were stationed a row of noble warriors on guard. These guards were highly impressed by the two wandering sisters. Little did they know that the young girls were quite terrified and extremely nervous. What the men saw were two beautifully-clad ladies adorned in precious jewels and carrying a thin rod that glowed inexplicably in the shadows. Paying them high honours, they bid the travellers to enter the compound, offered them a nourishing meal and showed them into a hut where they could rest for the night.

The next morning they approached the king of that land, announcing that 'Two princesses from an unknown country entered your kingdom last night.'

'Perhaps they have descended from the gods in the sky,' said the king. 'For this very day I have been praying for beautiful wives to wed my two sons. Arrange for an audience and I shall make preparations for the weddings!'

The king, of course, did not know that it was the magic wand that had directed Chichinguane and her sister (now disguised as elegant princesses) to his land. And he never would.

5
Folk Stories

Blaming it on Adam

The king in a Yoruba town lives in a palace similar to other houses but larger and more decorated, made up of a compound of several sets of rooms and outhouses. The marketplace is usually in front of his door. The biblical story of Adam was adapted in Nigeria so that the Garden of Eden was said to have 'plenty cassava, plenty banana, plenty yam, plenty mango' and so on. Eve stole a mango, not an apple, and Adam told God that she had used it in a groundnut stew. Clearly Adam's fault had made a great impression on Iyapo in this story.

Long ago there was a poor woodcutter named Iyapo who lived on the edge of the village in a small hut. Every morning he would get up early and go far away to the forest. In the forest, he would chop wood until the sun was at its highest point. Then he would carry all his wood down to the town and, after giving a few sticks to the tollkeeper at the gate, he would sell his wood.

He was always hungry but he had to sell his wood or he could not buy anything to eat.

Folk Stories

'Wood, wood. Good wood. Who'll buy some of my wood,' he would say as he walked up and down the streets. 'It's all the fault of Adam. Good wood for sale.' And so he sold some wood and bought food.

One day as Iyapo was selling his wood, the king heard him.

'Who is this person?' he asked his chief adviser. 'And why does he say that it's all the fault of Adam? If someone has wronged him then I should know about it.'

The chief adviser of the king asked all the other officers but none of them knew who he was or what he meant. So they took him to the king. He fell on the floor in respect.

'Now then, woodcutter, what is your name?' asked the king.

'Sire,' replied the frightened man, 'my name is Iyapo.'

'Iyapo, that name means "many troubles". But why are you blaming Adam?'

'I have heard that long ago Adam disobeyed God and ate the forbidden fruit. If he had not, we would all now be living in the Garden of Eden and I would never go hungry. That is why I say it is the fault of Adam.'

'I see,' said the king, looking thoughtfully at the woodcutter. 'You are a hard worker yet you go hungry. It does not seem fair that you are suffering because of Adam's mistake. I will help you.' The king called his chief adviser over and said to him, 'Have Iyapo properly washed and dressed. Bring him to the palace and let him stay in one of the rooms there. Take his rags and wood away and let him have a new life.'

He then said to Iyapo, 'From now on, you can call me brother. We will share everything and you can do anything you like except' – here he stared right into Iyapo's eyes – 'except, you may not open the green door at the end of the hall. That is the one thing that you must never do.'

'Oh, my king,' cried an ecstatic Iyapo, 'what reason do I have to open the green door. I have food, clothes and shelter, what more could I want?'

And so the woodcutter led his new life of comfort. He never had to get up early or work hard, indeed he had forgotten what it used to be like to get up every day and chop wood. He was eating very well and was even starting to get fat.

He had quite forgotten all about the green door. Then one day he happened to pass by it, and as he did he remarked to himself, 'That is the door which I must never open. Still, I wonder what is behind it that I, the king's brother, am not allowed to find out.' And with a sigh he carried on.

During the next few days Iyapo seemed to be drawn towards the door all the time. Without being aware of trying, he found himself outside the door several times a day and each time he was getting more and more curious as to what was behind it. Sometimes without thinking about it, his hand actually started towards the handle but he managed to stop himself each time.

One day, the king said to Iyapo, 'Brother, I have been called away to another town and I am afraid that I will not be back until much later in the day. I am entrusting the palace to you. Please make sure nothing happens.'

After the king left, the woodcutter started thinking, 'The king has given me the responsibility of the palace. That is correct, after all am I or am I not the brother of the king. So surely I am responsible for the room behind the green door as well. I must be. I am going straight there now to find out what is hidden there.'

After checking that no one was looking, he put his ear against the door. He could not hear anything.

'I simply have to know what is in there. I will just open it a crack and close it again. The king will never find out.' And so he opened the door very slightly. The room was dark but after a while he could see that all that was in there were the old rags he used to wear and the wood he used to sell. Then suddenly, a mouse ran out the door.

'Oh no,' cried Iyapo, 'the king was hiding a mouse in the room and now it has escaped. I must catch it.' And so he ran off in pursuit. As he ran, his shoes fell off. He started tripping over the bottom of his long, fancy robes and had to take them off. But still he could not catch the little mouse. His pampered life had made him fat and unfit and he was getting hot and out of breath. But he kept going – the king must not find out about his opening the door.

Suddenly the king was there. He was back early!

'And what are you doing, Iyapo?' boomed the king. 'Why are you running around the palace without your clothes. Such behaviour does not become someone in your high position. Get up.'

But the poor Iyapo was prostrate on the floor sobbing. 'I am sorry my king. I did not mean to let your mouse go.'

'What mouse?' asked the king. 'I have no mouse.'

'The mouse in the room. You see I just opened the green door for a…'

'You opened the green door?'

'It was a mistake. I did not mean to, but my feet kept taking me there and I was curious and…'

'Iyapo, I am very disappointed in you. Opening the green door was the one thing I told you not to do.'

'I know sire, but I am the brother of the king and…'

'And now you want to be the king yourself,' shouted the king, angrily. 'You are worse than Adam. You should have learned from his mistake.'

'I am sorry, my lord. It will never happen again, I promise. I am at your mercy, master. What do you wish of me?'

The king's mood had changed and now he had tears in his eyes.

'Go back to the room,' he said sadly, 'and take your rags and sticks. Return to the market and sell your wood.'

'Yes, sire.' The woodcutter could hardly speak.

'Just remember this, others cannot make you happy. It is up to you and your fate. Go and work hard and know that your poverty is not the fault of Adam or anyone else.'

And so Iyapo returned to the market and shouted, 'Good wood. Wood here. Who wants to buy good wood?' But no longer did he say anything about Adam.

The Snake Bite

Magic potions, like the powder in this story, are still very much part of Yoruba life today.

Once, in a small village there was a farmer who lived beside the main path. Everyone liked the farmer because he always kept a basket full of food by the side of the path. So when a tired friend or neighbour would pass by they could take a fruit or a yam or something else equally tasty.

Because of this whenever someone passed by the farm they would call him Ashoremashika which means The Man Who Always Does Good and Never Does Evil. When he heard this praise, he would call out to them and invite them to take something from the basket. And so everyone loved him in return.

After a while, a wicked man in the village began to get very jealous of the farmer whom everyone liked so much. He decided not only to stop him from being liked so much but also to make him hated ever after by the village people. So he found a poisonous snake in the grass and took it with him down the path.

'Good morning, Ashoremashika,' called the wicked man. 'I hope you are having a nice day.'

'I am, thank you,' replied the farmer. 'Please take something from my basket, my friend.' But instead of taking something, the man put the snake in the bottom of the basket. He then walked on a bit and hid in the bushes to watch.

Shortly a messenger came along with a message for the king. He was exhausted and called out to Ashoremashika who told him to take something from the basket. The jealous man was listening to all this with evil anticipation. Then he heard a scream and ran to the scene. He saw the farmer standing over the body of the messenger. The poor man was on the ground and clearly in pain. He was clutching his wrist which had a snake bite on it.

'Oh, Ashoremashika,' gasped the dying man, 'I have always been your friend. Why do you now try to kill me?'

'What do you mean?' asked the farmer in surprise.

'You put a snake in the basket to kill him,' accused the evil man who was by now right next to Ashoremashika. 'You will be executed for this.'

There was nothing the farmer could do to convince the other two of his innocence. He realized that the words of the newcomer were all too true and he would be executed before long. Still he was concerned for the messenger and carried him to the village doctor. But despite the doctor's best efforts the man died and Ashoremashika was arrested.

Although all the villagers wanted to believe that he was not guilty, the evidence was clear. There was the witness and the bite marks on the messenger's wrist were clear for everyone to see.

'All this time he has been nothing more than a murderer and a deceiver,' they said. 'How could we ever have trusted him?'

He was thrown in prison but as luck would have it the king's daughter was getting married and his execution was put off. After a few hours in his cell, Ashoremashika heard a hissing noise. Then with great surprise, he saw the very same snake which had bitten the messenger slither into his cell. The snake dropped a packet from his mouth onto the floor and spoke to the astonished farmer.

'Listen to me,' it said, 'I know that you are innocent and I will help you to prove it. Tonight, I will bite the princess and she will appear to be dead. However, this packet contains a medicine which can save her. Tell the king that you will bring his daughter back to life on the condition that you get your freedom. But you will tell him that the medicine will only work if it is mixed with the blood of a murderer. Use the blood of the evil man who is really guilty and the princess will awaken.' And with that the snake left.

The next day the whole palace was in mourning. During the whole of the day every doctor in the land tried in vain to bring life back to the princess. The king had just about given up hope when word got to him that Ashoremashika claimed to be able to save her. He sent for the farmer to be released and brought to him.

'Your majesty, this powder will bring your daughter back to life if mixed with the blood of a murderer. So I will now mix half of this medicine with my blood,' he said. He did so and put the mixture on the wound but nothing happened.

'So,' cried the king, angrily, 'you have tricked me.'

'No, not at all,' protested Ashoremashika. 'It does not work because I am not a murderer. The real murderer is the witness who was present when the messenger was dying. Allow me to take some of his blood and the princess will be alive shortly.'

The king agreed and called the man over, ordering him to give some of his blood to Ashoremashika. The farmer then mixed it with the other half of the powder and put it on the wound. The princess immediately opened her eyes and sat up.

With great surprise the evil minded man found himself thrown in a prison cell. Seeing that he was doomed, he gave a full confession and was shortly executed. Ashoremashika was released and he went back to the pathside to return to his old life.

A Quarrel Between Friends

(*Yoruba*)

There were once two very good friends called Olaleye and Omoteji. They both had farms next to each other and every day they would talk to each other. It was well known that they were best friends but one neighbour decided to test their friendship. He made himself a hat which was red on one side and green on the other. Then he set off down a path which passed between the two farms.

Folk Stories

After walking down the path for a while, he passed Omoteji on his left. 'Good morning, Omoteji,' he said.

'Good morning,' the farmer replied. 'What a nice new red hat that is you are wearing.'

'Thank you very much. I will see you later.' And with that he carried on down the path.

A little later on, he saw Olaleye on his left, weeding his yams. 'Good morning Olaleye, how are you today?'

'Oh, good morning,' he replied. 'I am fine. Say, I like your green hat.'

'Thank you, I made it myself, you know. Anyway, goodbye for now, Olaleye.'

He carried on his walk happy that his test had succeeded.

Soon it was lunch time and the two friends sat together by the path and ate. They talked about many different things before Olaleye spoke.

'Did you see our friend's new green hat this morning? He said that he made it himself.'

'Don't you mean red hat?' corrected Omoteji.

'No it was definitely green. You must have had the sun in your eyes or something.'

'But I made a remark to him about his red hat and he did not say it was green. So you must be the one who is mistaken.'

'I talked to him about it as well and it was definitely green.'

The argument became more and more heated and both insisted that they knew what colour the hat really was. Soon Omoteji got so irritated that he grabbed the other farmer by his neck. Olaleye was so angry that without thinking he punched Omoteji.

Before the fight could carry on, the neighbour returned. 'Why are you fighting?' As he said this he walked between the two so that each farmer saw the other side of the hat from the one that they had seen that morning.

They immediately stopped fighting. 'Oh my friend,' said Omoteji, 'you were right. I am sorry. The hat is green.'

'No, you were right. It is red.'

They would have probably started fighting again if their neighbour had not taken his hat off and showed them.

'My friends, please stop. My hat is both colours, see? But that is not important. What is important is that you cannot even discuss a simple thing like the colour of a hat without it turning into a fight.'

'Omoteji,' said Olaleye, 'I am sorry. I have been very foolish. I can see now that you can only know how good a friendship is after it has been tested. This will never happen again. From now on all I care about is having a good friend like you.'

'And I agree,' replied Omoteji. 'We will never again fight and we will be the best friends that ever existed.'

Indeed, from that day on they never came to blows again.

The Jealous King

Yoruba Kings are not hereditary: they are chosen by the council of elders of a town, who themselves are responsible for the town's administration. Sometimes, if the King behaves very badly, they have the power to force him to commit suicide, which is probably what happened at the end of this tale.

Once there lived a powerful but arrogant king. In the town that the king ruled there was a man who had called himself No-King-Is-as-Great-as-God. When the king heard about him he immediately wanted to punish this person who had dared to suggest that the king was not the most powerful person.

The king had to think hard of a way to harm No-King-Is-as-Great-as-God. After all the man had not done anything wrong. There was no law against anyone stating their beliefs and that was all that he had done. But the king was determined and finally came up with a plan that would make people forever laugh at the name No-King-Is-as-Great-as-God. And so very shortly the king summoned him to the palace.

'Now then,' asked the king, 'what is your name?'

'My name is No-King-Is-as-Great-as-God, master.'

'I understand that you chose this name for yourself. Does that mean that you believe that no king is as great as god?'

'Indeed it does, sire.'

'I see,' said the king. 'Well we will soon find out if you are right. But you are obviously a very brave and truthful man. Therefore, I will give you this ring as a symbol of our friendship. Take good care of it as it has been in my family for many generations and it is very precious to me. If you lose it I will take that to mean that you no longer value our friendship.'

'Fear not sire,' replied No-King-Is-as-Great-as-God, 'for I shall guard it with my life.' With that he put the ring in his deepest pocket and left the palace. He went straight home and told his wife what had happened.

But she was not pleased at all. 'My dear husband,' she said, 'can't you see that the king is just trying to find a way of harming you. He obviously does not like your name because he thinks that he is as great as God and I think he will try to kill you. You must take extra special care of this ring or your life will be in danger.'

No-King-Is-as-Great-as-God agreed with his wife and so together they tried to think of a safe hiding place for the ring. Eventually they dug a hole in the wall of their hut and put the ring in there. They then covered it up and smoothed it over and finally they hung a mat over the place.

As time went on, the king would often send for No-King-Is-as-Great-as-God. Sometimes they would have dinner together and sometimes they would just talk. But all the time the king tried to make No-King-Is-as-Great-as-God think that he was best friends with him. But No-King-Is-as-Great-as-God was not fooled and was always on the lookout for any trick the king might have up his sleeve.

His wife was equally worried, 'My dear, I am getting very concerned. The king certainly has a plan to kill you. Please do not go to the palace anymore.'

'But if I did not accept the king's invitations,' replied No-King-Is-as-Great-as-God, 'he would take that as an excuse to arrest me. From now on we must do anything we can to keep the king happy.'

One day a messenger from the king arrived at the house of No-King-Is-as-Great-as-God. His wife was home on her own and he told her that the king wished to see her. So she went with the messenger to the palace.

The king greeted her and said, 'I am planning a surprise for your husband. As you know he and I are almost like brothers and I would like us to wear matching rings. Do you think that you could give me his ring for me to have it copied?'

The woman was in a dilemma. She had to talk to her husband first but she did not know when he was to return. If she did not give the ring to the king now he might think that it had been lost.

Seeing that she was having trouble deciding what to do, the king told her, 'I have your husband's best interests at heart. The only reason I want the ring before he gets back is because I want it to be a surprise. Will you not do this to please your king?'

Then the woman remembered that her husband had told her to please the king in any way she could. So she went to the house and dug up the ring and, bringing it back to the palace, gave it to the king. Later on, when No-King-Is-as-Great-as-God came home, his wife decided not to tell him what she had done with the ring.

A couple of weeks later when No-King-Is-as-Great-as-God was at the palace, the king asked him to show him the ring.

'But sire,' he said, 'that ring is far too valuable for me to wear it all the time. I keep it in a very safe place.'

But the king was not pleased. 'So you do not value our friendship enough even to wear the ring. Does it embarrass you to wear something that was given to you by the king? You should show it off.'

'I am sorry. If you wish I will wear it at all times. I did not mean to offend you.'

'I think you are lying,' shouted the king, angrily. 'You do not have the ring any more. You have probably sold it. I challenge you to bring me that ring within seven days. If you can you may ask me for anything. You may even ask me for my life. But if you cannot show it to me, then your punishment will be terrible indeed.'

'If that is your wish,' replied the confident man, 'then so be it.' He walked back home very happy and sure that he would soon be able to ask something from the king. But at that very same moment, the king was throwing the ring into the sea.

When he got home he told his wife, 'We were right, the king has used the ring to try and kill me. But he has not succeeded. He thinks that I have lost the ring but it is still there in the wall, isn't it my dear?'

But his wife had started to cry. 'I am sorry my husband but while you were away the king tricked me into giving him the ring. We don't have it any more, he does.'

'Well then,' murmured the downcast man, 'it is hopeless.'

Suddenly his wife stopped crying. 'What is your name?' she asked.

'You know as well as I do that my name is No-King-Is-as-Great-as-God.'

'Exactly, and you believe that it is true, right?'

'Well of course I do. Why?'

'If you believe that God is greater than any king then you should just leave it up to God. After all everything that happens is decided by God anyway.'

And so No-King-Is-as-Great-as-God decided to celebrate with a feast. Even if he was to die, he was not going to waste his last few days. So he invited all his friends and neighbours. He then went with his wife to the market and bought several of the best fish. They took them back to their house and started to prepare the meal. But when one of the fish was cut open, they found their very own ring. They were very surprised but did not waste any time in burying it in the wall again.

The next day they had their feast and there was much music and dancing and singing. The celebrations went on well into the night and the king was amazed to hear so much joy from a man who was certain to die in less than a week. When the next day the king got a message from No-King-Is-as-Great-as-God saying 'There is definitely no king as great as God' he went mad with rage. He was looking forward to the time when he could kill this man who dared to challenge him like this. But the king noticed that the celebrations at the house of No-King-Is-as-Great-as-God went on for the next few days and he was very surprised.

When the seventh day came, the king wanted to make his triumph all the better by inviting all the townspeople to the palace. With just one hour to go of the seven days, No-King-Is-as-Great-as-God and his wife entered the palace along with a group of drummers and a group of dancers.

Just to make sure that everyone present knew what the challenge was, the king repeated it. 'If No-King-Is-as-Great-as-God can show me the ring now, I will give him anything he asks for. But if he cannot, I will execute him.' Then, laughing, the king asked him to show the ring.

Without saying a word, No-King-Is-as-Great-as-God reached into his pocket and pulled out the ring. The king's expression suddenly changed to one of complete horror. The only way that the ring could have got there was by the hand of God and the king knew it.

No-King-Is-as-Great-as-God had no hesitation in choosing what to ask of the king. He asked for his life. The king was executed and within the hour the town had a new king, No-King-Is-as-Great-as-God.

Folk Stories

The Reward of Envy

This striking morality tale introduces the Babalawo, learned priest and diviner for the god Orunmila, on whose oracles depended agricultural success, especially through rain-making ceremonies. Sometimes there would be several Babalawo in a single village.

(Yoruba)

There were once two friends who worked together in a shop. One of these two was more hard-working and was soon promoted to a higher position while the other stayed where he was. After a time the lazy man became very jealous of his friend. His jealousy played on his mind until he began to hate the man who had once been his friend and wish him dead. One day he decided to visit the Babalawo and ask for some spell to kill his friend.

When the native priest heard that his visitor wanted to kill someone just because he was jealous of the other man's success, he was reluctant to get involved.

'Listen to me,' he explained, 'what you want to do is wrong. This man is innocent – he has done you no harm. If you kill him, you will bring evil upon yourself.'

But the jealous man was determined and insisted he had been wrongly treated by his former friend. The priest at last relented and agreed to help him.

'All right, take this packet of poisonous powder and place it under the cushion on the man's chair. When he sits on it, his body will start to decay. It will happen gradually and he will spend a few days in bed dying slowly. However, his mind will not be affected so he will be able to think about his misery the whole time. But I warn you, this is powerful poison, and you should not use it without thinking carefully about the consequences.'

The evil-minded man was very pleased and took the packet. The next day he went to work much earlier than normal. Checking there was no one about, he put the packet on the chair of his old friend who he hated so much. He then started to tidy the shop with extra enthusiasm – he even tidied the shelves, which he would never normally have done – trying to look innocent and industrious while he waited for the other man to arrive. Shortly, his former friend came into the workshop.

'I am surprised to see you here at this time, my friend,' exclaimed the newcomer. 'You must want to be promoted, you are coming in so early and working so hard.'

But as he watched his lazy friend working with such uncharacteristic energy, he thought he had a guilty look about him. He suspected something was wrong. So when he was invited by the guilty man to sit at his desk, he decided not to. Instead he invented an errand to send him on. Although the jealous man didn't want to miss the moment when his old friend sat on the poisonous packet, he had to go because the other man was his superior, and he didn't want to raise any suspicions.

As soon as he was alone, the hard-working man looked around the shop to find what mischief his friend had done. But he could see nothing unusual. Then he noticed the cushion on his chair had been disturbed. He picked it up to rearrange it and saw beneath it the packet. He didn't know what it was, but guessed his friend must have put it there, and that it meant no good. So he put it under the cushion of his friend's chair, then sat down in his own seat.

Just then the envious man came back from his errand. He saw with satisfaction that his former friend was sitting down, and wondered how long it would take for the magic to have its effect. Not suspecting anything, he sat down in his own chair to start work. A few minutes after sitting down, he began to feel a slight dizziness followed by an unusual pain. Slowly it dawned on him that all was not well. He suspected that the packet was under his cushion, but he dared not look in front of his friend. So he had to sit on it as if nothing was wrong until lunchtime, when everyone would go off to eat. By the time lunch came he was in extreme pain. As soon as he was alone, he lifted the cushion and saw the packet. In horror he ran all the way to the native priest and begged him for help.

'I'm sorry, but there's nothing I can do for you,' said the priest. 'I warned you that no good would come of trying to kill an innocent person.'

The wretched man struggled home in agony. He could not find anything to relieve his pain. In despair he went to bed and stayed there for the last few days of his life. Although his body decayed hour by hour, his mind remained untouched and he had plenty of time to turn over in his mind how he had tried to kill his innocent friend.

The Suspect

This wise tale is from the mid-western region of Nigeria.

There was once a king who had a beautiful inlaid knife. It was forged by craftsmen of Benin and decorated with inlay of brass and copper. The king prized it as his best possession. One day a big carnival was held in his village. People came from far and wide to join in the festivities. There was dancing and singing and feasting, and the king gave out gifts. But when it was all over and everyone had gone home the king discovered that his precious knife was missing. He looked all over for it but couldn't find it anywhere. He suspected that someone at the carnival had stolen it.

Word was sent out all over the country that the king's inlaid knife was missing and a reward was offered to anyone who could find the thief. People were astonished.

'Who could be so foolish as to steal the king's knife?' they said, 'The thief must be found and punished.'

There was a particular village called Gbo. When the people of the village heard the news they looked around suspiciously. In the village was a hunter who lived alone. People questioned him.

'Weren't you at the king's carnival?'

'Yes,' he replied, 'I went there and ate and danced with everyone else. What of it?'

'You're a hunter, you need a knife don't you?'

'I have many weapons,' he answered. 'Why should I want to steal the king's knife? I wouldn't want to skin my animals with a knife belonging to the king.' The hunter didn't waste his time continuing the conversation and went off to hunt.

'Just see how he answers so sharply,' the people of the village said among themselves, 'He cannot be trusted. If he is innocent why does he look so angry? And he didn't want to talk about it and turned his back on us. Surely he has a guilty conscience. He must be the thief.'

As days and nights passed by, the people in the village began to watch the hunter with growing suspicion. When he went out into the forest in the morning, they watched him, and when he returned at dusk, they watched him.

'See how he walks, as if he had something to hide. He spends all his time in the bush and does not want to be seen. What does he do there all day?'

As time passed, everyone in the village became convinced that the hunter was the thief and no one would even talk to him any more. When he had skins to sell no one would buy them from him, so he had to take them to other villages. This made them even more suspicious. It seemed that whatever he did only incriminated him more. He started to spend days at a time in the forest and to come home after dark and not show his face in the village. Now they were certain that he was the thief.

'We should tell the king that we have found the one who stole his knife,' somebody said.

'But that would bring shame on our village,' said another. 'We should drive the hunter out, then we could report him, but still the king might be hard on us.' And so it went on.

One day a messenger arrived from the king's village. The knife inlaid with copper and brass had been found. It seemed that it hadn't been stolen after all. The king had hidden it in the rafters of his cottage and it had fallen down inside the grass wall. Everyone was relieved that the king's knife was found again and that it had not been stolen. The people of Gbo were especially pleased. Now they looked at the hunter with new eyes.

'Just see how hard he works. He spends all day in the bush and wastes no time. He is so determined that he will not return from the hunt until he has some game,' said one.

'He doesn't talk much, because he is so serious,' said another.

'And the way he walks – you can see he is afraid of nothing.'

'You only need look at him to see that he's an honest man.'

So the saying arose:

When the king's knife is stolen
The hunter walks like a thief.
When the king's knife is found
The hunter is praised.

The King's Magic Drum

Southern Nigeria (Yoruba)

There was an ancient King of Calabar called Efriam Duke. He was a peaceful man who did not like war. He had a wonderful possession – a magic drum. Whenever the drum was beaten it would provide enough good food and drink to feed everyone present.

Whenever there was threat of war from some belligerent neighbours, the king's strategy was simple. He would simply invite all his enemies together and sit them down. Then he would beat his drum and, instead of having a fight, they would find themselves surrounded by an extravagant feast. Everyone would eat and drink until their stomachs were full and their minds at peace, then they would make up their quarrels and leave as friends again.

At other times the king would invite all the village people and even the animals of the bush to join him for a feast. Everyone would assemble with great anticipation and watch as the king beat the drum. Then there would be feasting and merry-making all day and night. In those days there was no fear between animals and men, so they all celebrated together. In these ways the wise King Efriam kept his domain peaceful and prosperous.

There was only one problem with the drum, which was known only to the king. If its owner chanced to walk over a fallen tree trunk, or even a broken branch lying on the path, the spell of the drum would immediately be broken, and instead of food appearing, three hundred Egbo men armed with sticks and whips would appear and beat the owner of the drum and any invited guests very severely. However, the king was very careful to avoid stepping over any fallen tree trunks or branches, so all was well. Everyone envied him his drum and wished they could have it for themselves, but naturally the king would under no circumstances part with it.

King Efriam was a wealthy man. He had many beautiful wives who each had plenty of healthy children. One morning one of the king's wives took her little daughter to the spring for a wash. A tall palm tree full of ripe palm nuts grew over the spring, and it so happened that Tortoise was up the tree gathering palm nuts for his lunch. Accidentally he let one of the nuts fall to the ground. The little girl saw the palm nut roll along the ground beside her and cried out hungrily. Her mother, not realizing it came from Tortoise, gave it to her. Tortoise, seeing what had happened, climbed down from the tree and asked the king's wife to return his palm nut.

'How can I give it to you,' she replied, 'I have given it to my daughter to eat.'

'I am a poor person,' argued Tortoise, 'and I have a family to feed. Do you think that I can afford to give away my palm nuts just because your daughter decides she is hungry? I will go and report this matter to the king. Let's see what he has to say when he hears that one of his wives has stolen my food.' In the bush it is considered a serious crime to steal another's food.

'I had no idea the palm nut was yours. I saw it lying on the ground and gave it to my daughter. I have done no wrong, but if you have a complaint against me or my child I have nothing to fear. My husband is a rich man, and I will take you to him.'

So when the mother had finished washing her child she brought Tortoise before her husband the king, where Tortoise made a lot of fuss, complaining bitterly about the loss of his palm nut. The king listened patiently to Tortoise's story and then offered to compensate him for the loss of the nut.

'What would you like me to give you? You can have anything you choose: money, clothes, palm oil, more palm nuts.' But Tortoise refused all the king's offers. There was only one thing he wanted.

'Give me your magic drum.'

'This drum is my most valuable possession. But I am bound to give you what you ask for. Take it!' The king was exasperated with Tortoise, so in order to get rid of him, he agreed to let him take the drum, but he did not tell him the most important thing about it – what would happen if its owner stepped over a fallen tree or branch. That remained the king's secret.

As soon as Tortoise carried the drum to his home in the bush, he called together his wife and children.

'Let's celebrate! The king has given me his magic drum. We need never go short of food again. Any time we want we can have a feast, and we can invite all the people of the village to join us, and make them our friends.' So he beat the drum in the same way as he had seen the king do when he wanted something to eat and immediately a fabulous spread of food and drink appeared before them which they ate and drank to their heart's content.

For three successive days Tortoise and his family feasted with the help of the drum, and they all became sleek and well-fed. Then he issued invitations to all the people of the village to come and join them for a big feast. People laughed when they received their invitations because everyone knew that Tortoise was poor and never entertained guests, so very few guests turned up. But the king, knowing about the magic drum, came with all his family, and a few others attended, and they all enjoyed their meal very much.

The next day news spread about Tortoise's newly found wealth and the quality of his food. Everyone resolved to accept his invitation if it came again. Tortoise, feeling very pleased with himself, took his drum for a walk in the forest. While walking along the forest path, unaware of the king's secret, he stepped over a fallen branch. At the time nothing happened, but the drum's spell was broken. When he got home his wife asked him to beat on his drum, because the family was hungry. He beat on the drum, and to his dismay three hundred Egbo men appeared and began to beat him and his family without mercy for a long time. At last they vanished and left the family to nurse their wounds. Tortoise, once he had recovered, could understand that somehow the spell had been broken. He felt very bitter at being so cheated and decided that he would get his own back on the whole village. Let them all suffer the same misfortune, he thought. So he issued another general invitation.

This time no one wanted to miss the occasion, and when it was time for the feast everyone from the village and surrounding area came to Tortoise's house. Only the king gave his excuses and with his family stayed away. When all was ready, Tortoise began to beat the drum, then he and his family quickly hid themselves. Instantly the three hundred Egbo men appeared armed with whips and sticks and began their relentless beating of all the guests, not allowing a single one to escape. At last the Egbo men vanished and those who could still walk made their escape, carrying on their backs those who were too badly hurt to use their legs.

After that everyone was so angry with Tortoise that he decided it would be wise not to show his face in the village for a while. As soon as he could, he begged the king to take back the drum, and all returned to normal in the kingdom of Efriam Duke.

How To Find Suffering

A sad story from the Alur.

Listen while I tell you the story of a man who wanted suffering, so that you may not make the mistake he made.

Once a man of the Alur tribe went to visit a friend of his who belonged to the Gungu tribe and lived beside Lake Albert. When he came upon his friend he found him smoking a pipe. As he smoked he blew out long wisps of coloured smoke into the air, that hung above him before drifting away in strange shapes. In those days, men thought pipes were very wonderful things, and that those who smoked them were specially wise, perhaps because the smoke spirits who wafted around them gave them ideas and insights.

'My friend, why do you smoke that pipe?' asked the man of the Alur tribe.

'I smoke because I have so many worries,' replied the Gungu man. 'It is my suffering which makes me smoke.'

The man of the Alur was most impressed, he wanted to have whatever his friend had.

'My friend, I don't have any of that suffering you speak of. I want what you have. Please let me have some of your suffering.'

The Gungu man remained silent for a while, smoking his pipe.

Then he seemed to make up his mind, and spoke.

'If you're sure that's what you want, it's easily arranged. Just send over your three sons to me tomorrow, and I will give them some suffering for you.'

The following morning he sent his three sons off to visit the man by the lake.

'Be careful on your journey,' he told them, 'and be sure not to come back without some suffering for me.' The boys went on their way and before long they reached the Gungu man's home.

'What did you come for?' asked the man. He wanted to be sure his friend really wanted this.

'We've come to collect some suffering to take home to our father,' they replied.

'Very well then,' declared the man, and went inside. He took a blackbird and put it in a box.

'Here, take this to your father,' he said, handing them the box, 'but don't look inside it!'

The boys set off home. On the way they grew tired so they sat down to rest. They were all curious to see their father's suffering. They couldn't resist opening the box to have a peep. So they opened the lid just a little bit. Suddenly, before they could prevent it, the blackbird flew out of the box, up into the sky and in a trice disappeared into the bush.

The boys were all agitated, and began to accuse each other.

'It was your fault,' said one, 'You opened the lid and let it escape.'

'No it was yours,' said another. 'You were the one who wanted to see your father's suffering in the first place.'

'It's both your faults,' said the third, 'I never wanted to open the box.'

Soon a fight started. It got more and more violent. The boys got hurt, which made them even more angry, so they fought on. Eventually all of them lay dead on the path.

Late afternoon came, and still the boys had not returned. Their father was worried and set off along the road to see what had become of them. After some time he came upon their dead bodies strewn across the path, beside them the empty box. As the sun sank over the horizon he dropped to his knees in grief. As he knelt there crying aloud, the Gungu man came along the road from the other direction, and saw what had happened.

'What is the matter?' he asked.

'My children, whom I sent to you to collect some suffering for me, have lost my suffering. They must have quarrelled, and now see what has become of them. They have killed each other.'

'My friend,' said the Gungu man, 'what escaped from the box was not suffering. You asked me for suffering and now you have it, but it has overwhelmed you. One does not ask for suffering.'

Remember this story and the lessons it teaches. Be careful of those who smoke pipes – their brains are too big and their hearts are full of sad memories. Never ask for something you don't understand – be satisfied with what you have. And don't open strange boxes which do not belong to you.

The Girl Who Wanted Dawn's Dress

(Alur)

A beautiful young girl once lived with her aunt in a village by a lake. Because she was so beautiful, many of the young men in the village wanted to marry her. She was beautiful, but she was also proud. Whenever one of the young men asked for her hand in marriage she replied disdainfully that she would only marry the man who could bring her the red dress of dawn as her bride-price. None of them knew what kind of magic was required to get the red dress of dawn, so each had to go away disappointed.

One day a young man from another village approached her with more than usual determination. When she gave him her usual bride-price he thought what to do. The girl's aunt was a wise woman, and she knew her niece well, so he decided to ask for her help. First, however, the young man set about befriending the old woman and gaining her trust.

Now she was a curious old woman, even more wilful than the girl, and it was her habit to eat only dung instead of solid food. In front of her hut was always to be found a pile of dung, making quite a smell, and people in the village were quite rude about it. The young man, however, took no notice of this and when he went to see her he greeted her in the most polite way possible.

'Hello young man, it is kind of you to speak to me. Please do me a favour. I have to go now to the fields to pick their fruits.' She meant she was going to gather more dung. 'While I am gone can you please wait here and guard my food?' So saying she pointed to the dung heap before her cottage and left.

The young man patiently sat in front of the house watching over her food. The smell was unpleasant, but he reassured himself by thinking about all the dangers and hardships he had taken in the bush when he was hunting. Now he was seeking a far greater prize so should he not be prepared to put up with some little difficulties?

While he was waiting it began to rain, so he moved inside for shelter. Then he realized that if it carried on the rain would wash away the pile of dung. He had been asked to guard it, and he thought to himself that he could not just sit there and allow it to be washed away – the old woman would be most upset. So, although the bad smell disgusted him, he used his bare hands to carry it, handful by handful, inside the hut out of the rain.

Just as he finished this task the woman returned. Seeing what he had done she was very pleased with him.

'No one else even speaks a polite word to me,' she said. 'But you have been polite and kind, and now you have gone to great lengths to look after my food. Let me do something for you. I will prepare you a meal – something that you will like.'

So she cooked him a dish which was considered a special delicacy in those parts: millet with ants. As he ate she sat down beside him and asked why he had come to see her. He told her he wanted her advice on how to woo her niece.

'Normally I wouldn't tell this to a young man, but you have been very considerate. Now here's what to do,' she began. 'Go and ask the girl to sleep with you. Tell her that she should sleep by your feet and you by hers – then she will agree. In the morning when the cock crows, give her this unground millet and tell her to make porridge from it. She will do her best to obey you, and then you will know what to say.'

Overjoyed, the young man went and found the girl and asked her to sleep with him as the old lady had advised. The girl agreed. So they spent the night side by side, her by his feet and he by hers. As the cock crowed, he got up and gave the millet to the girl.

'I want you to make me some porridge.'

'But this millet is unground – I will need flour,' she protested.

'In my village the women make porridge from millet like this. If you are clever you will be able to do it.'

So she tried to cook porridge, but found it impossible. Perplexed, she came back to the young man, just as the sun was rising into a red sky.

'I can't do it – you show me how.'

'Ah – you admit that you cannot do it, and no wonder. The women of my village can't either – they grind their millet just like everyone else. Yet you demand me to get you the red dress of dawn – tell me how I am to do that! Can you show me?'

'I have nothing to say. I don't know how it is to be done,' said the girl. 'Your words are true. You have outwitted me. I promise that I will marry you.'

Chief Liongo

(Swahili)

In ancient times, Shanga was a flourishing village with a large population. One of its most prominent citizens was Liongo, a man of great strength and power. Unfortunately, he oppressed the people excessively, until one day they devised a plan to ambush him in his hut and bind him. So it was that a great number of people went and came upon him without warning in his hut where they seized and bound him. Then they took him to a cave in the hills and therein locked him up.

For many days Liongo remained in the cave until finally he was able to break his bonds and escape from it. So he went beyond the village boundary and began to harass the people for many weeks, just as he had done before. It became impossible for the villagers to go out into the fields, neither could they cut wood in the forest nor draw water from the river. And great sorrow fell upon them.

And the people said among themselves: 'What strategy can we resort to in order to trap Liongo and kill him?'

'Let us pounce on him while he is asleep,' said one man. 'Then we can get rid of him forever and we shall have our former peace.'

'Go ahead, if you think you can do it,' said the others. 'But do not kill him. Only bind him and bring him into the village.'

So a select group armed themselves one evening and waited until nightfall outside Liongo's hut. When he had fallen asleep they pounced on him and bound him with chains so strong that he could never smash them. After this, they brought him fettered into the centre of the village. And there he was made to stand with a post between his legs.

Liongo was left like this for many days and all the villagers would pass by him ridiculing and taunting him. The only person that took pity on him was his mother, who used to send him food every day. But there where he was bound, sentries were posted. They kept watch day and night, never leaving him except when it was time to change the guard.

Many weeks and many months passed and Liongo, in order to pass the time of day, would sing very beautiful songs. Everyone who heard them was amazed and delighted by his mellow voice and the melodious songs. It was not uncommon for someone to say to his friend, 'Let us go this evening and listen to Liongo's beautiful songs which he sings in the village centre.' And they would go and listen. These songs were actually improvized by Liongo himself and they became very popular, delighting all the listeners. Every evening an audience would gather around the captive in order to be entertained.

'We have come to hear some of your songs,' they would say. 'Please sing for us.' And sing he would; he could not refuse for the people of the village were gladdened by them. In fact, every single day Liongo composed new and different tunes because he was grieved at being held fast by chains and music gave him some respite. Gradually the villagers began to learn the songs and sing them at home to their children. But few really understood their inner meaning. Only he, his mother and her slave girl appreciated their essence; the other people did not.

One winter's day the slave girl brought some food for Liongo from his mother. But the guards snatched it from the girl and ate it, leaving behind only a few scraps which they returned to her. The slave girl told her master what had happened: 'I brought food for you from your mother but the guards took it from me and ate it. All that remain are these scraps.'

'Give them to me,' he said to her. And he gathered them into his cupped hands and ate them, thanking the gods for what he had received.

Then he lifted up his voice and sang a new song to the slave girl, a song with a special meaning for her and for his mother. The words went like this:

> They shall send you, O sweet slave girl,
> With a message for my aged mother:
> 'Your son is nothing but a simpleton,
> He knows not, even now, the ways of this world.'
> Let us show them, O sweet slave girl,
> Let us show them how they err.
> Have my mother bake a cake,
> And in the middle let files be placed.
> That I may cut my fetters,
> That I may break my chains,
> That once more I may take the road,
> That I may glide like a snake,
> That I may mount the roofs and walls,
> That I may look this way and that.

'Greet well my mother for me,' Liongo continued quietly, 'and tell her what I have told you.' And she went and told his mother, and said, 'Your son, Liongo, greets you well and he has given me a message to come and tell you.'

'What is the message?' asked the mother. And the slave girl told her about Liongo's new song.

Liongo's mother understood everything at once and hurried off to the granary where she bartered for some grain. She gave it to her slave girl to clean. Then the mother went and acquired a number of sharp files and brought them to her hut. And taking the flour she made many fine cakes. And taking the bran she made a plain, large cake. And taking the files she put them into it. She gave all of the cakes to her slave girl to take to her son.

And she went with them and arrived at the place where Liongo was bound. But once again the guards robbed her of her goods. Choosing only the fine cakes, the guards ate them greedily. But as for the large, plain bran cake, they told her to take that to her master. This she did; and he broke it to remove the concealed files. After hiding them in a secret spot, he ate the cake, drank some water and felt satisfied and refreshed.

Now the people of the village expressed the wish that Liongo be executed. And he himself heard them say, 'You must be done away with.' So he asked his guards, 'When do they plan to execute me?'

'Tomorrow,' was the blunt reply. And so he said, 'Grant me one last wish.'

'What is it?' they asked.

'Call to me my mother, and the chief ruler of the village, as well as all the village people, that I take my leave of them.'

'Your wish shall be granted,' said the guards. So they sent off a message and had everyone assemble before the ill-fated Liongo. The entire village population was there, including his mother and the slave girl.

And he asked them, 'Are you all assembled?'

'We are assembled,' they answered. So he said to them, 'I have need of a horn, and cymbals, and a drum.' And they went and fetched them.

'I have prepared an entertainment for you today,' he explained, 'for I need to take leave of you.' And they said to him, 'Very well, go on and entertain us.'

'Let one take up the horn, and another take up the cymbals, and a third take up the drum,' instructed Liongo.

'But how shall we play these things?' they cried. So there and then he taught them to play; and they played and played to their hearts' content.

Meanwhile, Liongo himself sang with a full and sonorous voice while the whole company made music with great enthusiasm and rejoicing. In the general confusion and merry making, the captive was able to draw out one of the files undetected and with it he began to cut his fetters. But at moments when the music began to die down, he left off cutting and restored the excitement and fervour of the celebration. Many of the villagers then took to dancing around the huts and farms. In this way, Liongo could resume his efforts at escape.

The people knew nothing of what was going on through their

delight in the entertainment that Liongo had provided. In due course, he had cut through his chains and fetters and without warning he appeared to them free of his bonds and obviously very incensed. Horrified, the people threw their instruments away and stopped their dancing. They attempted to escape by running off, but they were not quick enough; because he caught up with them, bashed their heads together and killed them. Then taking leave of his mother, he travelled to the outskirts of the village into the forest where he remained for many days, tormenting and beleaguering the people as before, and even killing them.

So the villagers devised another strategy to do away with him. They convinced a number of sly and devious men to go out and befriend Liongo in order to find an opportunity to destroy him. These men went out in great trepidation. And when they encountered him in the forest they made a truce and promised to be his friends. One day they said to him, 'Lord Liongo, let us divert and amuse one another.' To which Liongo replied, 'If I were to be cheered by your diversion, what could I give in return, I who am so very poor.' Then one of the others hit upon an idea: 'Let us entertain one another with koma fruit.' And Liongo asked him, 'How shall we eat them?'

'One of us shall climb into the koma tree,' he said, 'and throw them down for us to eat. When one has had his turn, another will climb up and do the same until we have all finished.'

'Very well,' said Liongo.

So the first climbed into the tree, and they ate. And the second climbed up, and they ate. And the third climbed up, and they ate. But the others had plotted that when Liongo's turn came to climb up, 'We shall shoot him down with arrows there, up above.'

But Liongo saw through their mischief for he was extremely wise. Thus when all had finished they said to him, 'Come now, it is your turn.' And he said, 'Very well.' And he took up his bow in his right hand, and his arrows, saying, 'With these I shall strike the ripest fruit of all that sit in the highest branches, and we shall eat in abundance.' Then he took aim and shot; a bough broke off and fell to the ground. And he shot again, and a second was broken off; in time the branches of the entire koma tree had been separated from the trunk and the ground was covered with fruit. Thus did they eat. And when they had finished, the men said among themselves, 'It is obvious that he has seen through our scheme; now what are we to do?'

'Let us be off from here,' they decided, 'before he tears us from limb to limb.' So they took their leave of him, saying, 'Lord Liongo, you have not been taken in; you are less a man and more a spirit, for like a demon you have tricked us with your guile.'

Thereupon the men went back to the village where they approached the ruler in order to make their report.

'We could do nothing,' they said. The counsellors assembled together.

'Who will be able to subdue this man?'

'Perhaps his nephew will,' suggested someone. And they went and called his nephew. And he came. And they said to him, 'Go to your uncle and ask him what it is that will kill him. When you know, come and tell us, and when he is dead we will give you all his inheritance.' And he answered them, 'Very well.'

And he went. When he arrived Liongo welcomed him and said, 'What have you come to do?' And he said, 'I have come to see you.' And he said, 'I know that you have come to kill me, and they have deceived you.' And the nephew asked him, 'Lord Liongo, what is it that can kill you?' And he said, 'A needle made from ivory. If anyone stabs me in the navel with an ivory needle, I die.'

So the nephew went back to the village and made his report to the ruler and to the counsellors, saying, 'It is a needle made from ivory that will kill him.' And they gave him such a needle, and he went back to Liongo. And when he saw his nephew, Liongo sang this new song:

I, who am bad, am he that is good to you.
Do me no evil.
I, who am bad, am he that is good to you.

Thus did Liongo welcome him, for he knew, 'He has come to kill me.'

The nephew remained with him for two days. At night on the second day Liongo fell asleep in his hut, and the nephew stabbed him in the navel with the ivory needle. Liongo awoke in agonizing pain, and taking his bow and arrows went to a place near the well. There he knelt down and propped himself up with his weapons. And that is how he died.

But in the morning the women of the village who came to draw water saw him, and they thought him to be alive. So they hastened back to their homes. And they gave out the news in the village: 'No water is to be had today.' Everyone else that went to the well came back running. For many people set out and went that way, and as they approached they saw Liongo. They imagined him to be alive so they immediately headed back, fearful of getting too close. And for three days the village people were in distress for water, not daring to come close to the well.

Finally they called Liongo's mother and said to her, 'Go and speak to your son, that he may go away so we can get water, or we will kill you.' And she went out to the well and came up to him. And his mother took hold of him to soothe him with songs, and he fell down at her feet. And his mother wept bitterly; for she knew her son was dead.

Returning to the village, she told the ruler and the counsellors that her son was dead, and they went to look at him, and saw that he was dead, and buried him, and his grave is to be seen at Ozi to this day.

Then they seized the young nephew and killed him and kept the inheritance for themselves.

6
Fables

The Antelope in the Moon

The theme of sacrificing one's mother in the time of famine is a common one in stories from Africa, where famine has been a constant fear. As in this Yoruba story, it often involves the deceit of a trickster.

Once, in ancient days, there was a famine. All the animals in the bush were crying with hunger, so they met together to decide what to do. Kiniun the lion sat and listened to what everyone had to say. There was no easy solution. Then Asa the hawk made a proposal. Each of them in turn should offer their mother to be eaten by the community. Everyone agreed that this was the only solution.

'So it shall be,' declared Kiniun. 'I appoint Etu the antelope to supervise the arrangements.'

Because Etu was given the honour of being in charge, he was to provide the first meat. But Etu had no intention of sacrificing his mother. Instead he led her to a secret place in the bush and climbed with her to the moon where he hid her. The moon was a place of plenty. The earth was corn flour with honey oozing from springs in the ground, and the houses were made from sweetbread. Etu told her to stay there until it was safe to return. He gave her a rope so that whenever he wanted to visit her she could lower it to earth and pull him up.

Etu returned to earth and gathered a pile of rotten wood from the forest. He cut it into small pieces, seasoned it with salt and pepper, and cooked it in oil. Then he brought it to the other animals with tears in his eyes.

'I have done what I had to do. Please eat what is left of my poor mother.'

All the animals began to eat and they enjoyed the food.

'Antelope meat tastes good,' they said.

One after another they all did what was required of them. The buffalo, the hawk, the elephant, even Kiniun the lion, killed their mothers and brought the meat to feed the rest. But still the famine went on, and everyone was hungry. The animals grew thin and desperate. Etu, however, regularly went to visit his mother on the moon, and there he ate as much as he wanted, so he did not grow thin.

Ijapa the tortoise noticed that Etu was growing fat. He was suspicious.

'How is it that when all the animals in the bush are getting thinner and thinner, you grow fat, Etu?' Etu remained silent, because he didn't trust Ijapa. But the tortoise kept on questioning him day after day. Eventually, Etu confided in him.

'If you come with me to the bush tomorrow, I will show you my secret.'

The next morning at sunrise Ijapa was waiting for Etu. The antelope led him to the secret place in the bush and sang to the moon.

Woman in the moon – alujan kijan!
Others have eaten their mothers – alujan kijan!
Even Kiniun the lion – alujan kijan!
Only I have not – alujan kijan!

Let down your rope – alujan kijan!
So I may come and eat – alujan kijan!

The antelope's mother let down her rope. Etu and the tortoise grabbed hold of it and she pulled them up to the moon. When they got there the tortoise wasted no time. He gorged himself on corn flour, honey and sweetbread until he could eat no more. Then they returned to earth. They walked back through the bush together and said goodbye. Ijapa went straight to Kiniun.

'Etu has cheated us,' he said. 'He hid his mother on the moon and has been going there to eat. That's why he's so fat. The moon is full of honey and bread.'

'The antelope would not cheat me,' replied the lion. 'It was I who appointed him in charge.'

'If I have not spoken the truth, you can cut off my head!'

'That is a serious thing you have said, Ijapa, so we shall all investigate your claim.'

Kiniun first called Etu and gave him a job to do.

'Take all the broken hoes to the town to be repaired,' he ordered. They were a heavy load and Etu set off slowly on his way to the town. Meanwhile the lion ordered all the animals to come with him and together they followed Ijapa into the bush. Ijapa led them to the spot where Etu had sang his song. Imitating Etu's voice, he sang.

Woman in the moon – alujan kijan!
Others have eaten their mothers – alujan kijan!
Even Kiniun the lion – alujan kijan!
Only I have not – alujan kijan!
Let down your rope – alujan kijan!
So I may come and eat – alujan kijan!

The antelope's mother lowered her rope and all the animals took hold of it. She began to pull them up, but they were very heavy. She managed to get them halfway but got tired and could pull them no further. There they stayed, dangling halfway between the moon and the earth.

When Etu returned from his journey he found the countryside deserted. He went into the bush and found the animals dangling from the rope. He called up to his mother to cut the rope. She cut it and they all came crashing down to earth. Some were killed and some were badly hurt.

Ijapa the tortoise smashed his shell into many pieces. He asked the cockroaches to mend it for him and they tried their best. Because they were too slow he beat them, and that is why cockroaches have flattened bodies even to this day. Eventually they managed to stick his shell together again, but the marks still show of where it was mended.

Antelope was not able to visit the moon any more, because the rope had been cut. So his mother is still up there waiting to come down. On some nights you can look up at the moon and see her up there where her son took her to be safe.

Tortoise and the Palm Tree

The marketplace figures prominently in this Yoruba story. The Yoruba people are fond of trading and the market, which takes place every four days or so, is an important social occasion. Goods are either bartered, or exchanged for cowrie shells or coins. The marketplace in this story must have served a region encompassing many villages. The Sigidi figure mentioned in the story is a deity of medicine, usually made from clay, used by the Babalawo priests.

There were once two friends, a farmer and a tortoise, who lived together very happily in a small village. The farmer spent most of his time looking after his fields of yams, corn, cassava and beans. Tortoise was no good at digging and hoeing, being slow and clumsy, but he did have a strong sense of smell. So he used to track down bush rats and rabbits. Then the farmer would come and lay traps for them. So one way or another, the two of them used to eat pretty well. Until one day the farmer died.

Tortoise didn't know what to do. On his own he couldn't grow anything in the fields, nor could he catch the bush rats and rabbits, because he didn't know how to trap them. How would he be able to eat? However, Tortoise was a shrewd fellow, who always managed to get what he wanted in the end. So he sat down to think about what to do.

As he thought he noticed that it was market day in the village. All around him people were walking to market carrying all sorts of produce. Some had corn and yams, some had cassava and beans, some carried palm oil, or firewood, or animal skins, or pots. They all had valuable things to sell at the market.

'Why should I sit here worrying,' said Tortoise, 'When the market will be full of so many good things. Friends will be meeting there, traders doing business, farmers exchanging news. Surely a hungry tortoise like me will be able to find something there to eat. But how will I get it if I have no money or nothing to barter with?'

So Tortoise thought and thought, and at last he came up with a plan.

When everyone had gone off to market and all was quiet, he made his way to a big old palm tree that grew near the marketplace. Carefully, while no one was looking, he crawled inside the hollow base of the tree and hid himself there. Then he began to sing softly to the tree:

Dance, palm tree, dance,
Dance all round the marketplace.
Dance, palm tree dance,
Dance across the ground.

And the old palm tree began to dance. Swaying this way and that, it danced right through the middle of the village and into the marketplace.

The people in the market were amazed – no one had ever seen a tree dance before. They thought there must be a ghost in the tree. In great fear and confusion they began running this way and that, panicking to get out of the way of the dancing tree. The market was transformed into a scene of chaos as everyone tried to get away. Mothers ran after children, men ran after wives, and soon all the people of the village had vanished, terrified of the tree. The marketplace was now empty, except for the dancing tree and inside it Tortoise softly singing – and of course all the corn, yams, beans, cassavas and other good things that in their haste the frightened people had left behind. Tortoise stopped singing. The old palm tree stopped dancing and stood still right in the middle of the marketplace.

Slowly Tortoise emerged. The market was silent and empty, except for great piles of lovely things to eat in all directions. He lost no time in gathering all that he could manage and taking it back to the tree where he got it all inside the hollow trunk and squeezed in himself. Then he started his song again.

> Dance, palm tree, dance
> Dance back through the marketplace.
> Dance, palm tree, dance,
> Dance back to your home.

And the old palm tree danced back to its normal place. There Tortoise waited patiently inside the tree. Gradually all the people crept back into the village, and seeing the tree back in its normal place, said to themselves it was safe again. Tortoise waited until nightfall, then he dragged his spoils to his home and had a huge feast, feeling very happy with himself.

Meanwhile, word reached the king of strange happenings in the village marketplace. A palm tree had danced, he was told, and everyone had run away in fear. How he laughed.

'You must all have drunk too much palm wine,' he said, 'I never heard such a ridiculous story.'

So the elders of the village decided perhaps the king was right and they should just forget about the whole thing. 'After all,' they said, 'nothing like this has ever happened before, so why should it ever happen again?'

After a few days it was time for market again. Tortoise had eaten all his supplies and was hungry. Once more he waited for the marketplace to fill up and secretly climbed back inside the hollow old palm tree. Again he began to sing.

> Dance, palm tree, dance,
> Dance all round the marketplace.
> Dance, palm tree dance,
> Dance across the ground.

And once again the old palm tree danced right through the middle of the village and into the marketplace, and again everyone panicked and ran away. Once more Tortoise was able to help himself to all the produce – this time he was more choosy – and take it all back to the hollow tree. Again he sang to the tree.

> Dance, palm tree, dance
> Dance back through the marketplace.
> Dance, palm tree, dance,
> Dance back to your home.

And the old palm tree danced back to its normal place where Tortoise waited patiently until nightfall before taking his booty home and having another huge feast.

This time there was uproar in the village. Many of the market people had lost their best produce and everyone was more frightened than ever. An official delegation was sent to the king to ask for his help. The king still didn't believe what he was told, but he did agree to send three of his messengers to the next market day, just to keep the villagers quiet.

Next market day Tortoise was hungry again. Off he went to the old palm tree and sang his song inside the hollow trunk. Meanwhile everyone was waiting in the marketplace to see what was going to happen, including the king's three messengers. Once more the palm tree came dancing along, and once more everyone fled in terror, with the king's messengers the last to run away, as befits messengers of the king.

That night, while Tortoise was feasting himself, the messengers were telling the king what they had seen.

'Believe us, what they say is true. We really did see a dancing palm tree.'

'Well I still don't believe this ridiculous story,' said the king, 'but I suppose I had better send my chief minister – he's someone I can trust.'

So next market day the chief minister was waiting with everyone else to see the dancing palm tree. Sure enough, with a hungry Tortoise singing his song inside, the old palm tree came dancing into the marketplace, sending the villagers running in all directions. The chief minister was very brave and waited almost until the tree had touched him before he was overcome with fear and ran off like everyone else.

The chief minister told the king what he had seen. This time the king took what he heard seriously.

'I suppose I had better go down there myself and see what's going on. At least I shan't be afraid like everyone else and run away. I'll stay there and get to the bottom of this.'

A few days later at the market, the king himself was there to witness the dancing tree. With him were his messengers and his chief minister and all the people of the village. Not suspecting any of this, Tortoise sang his song inside the hollow of the old palm tree, and the tree danced into the market. One by one all the people and the king's messengers and even his chief minister deserted him, until he was the only person left in the marketplace, while the old palm tree danced ever closer. The king thought to himself.

'I am the king, and kings are never afraid of anything. I cannot allow this dancing tree to frighten me away. I will stand my ground.' Nevertheless, as the tree got nearer and nearer his teeth began to chatter with fear until he could stand it no longer, and off he ran.

Angry and humiliated, the king vowed that he would do something to stop this. He sent out a proclamation that anyone who could rid the village of the dancing tree, and solve the mystery of the missing food, would get a rich reward.

Now, there was a wise old man who had heard all about the events in the village and knew exactly what was going on and what to do. He came and told the king that he could solve his problem.

The old men came to the village the day before the next market day. All day long he laboured to make a curious life-size image of a man. The image looked so lifelike that all who saw it expected it to move and speak. It was called Sigidi. The next morning the king and all the people joined the old man in the marketplace. Sigidi stood right in their midst and the old man covered it with a coating of amo, a substance so sticky that anything which touches it sticks fast. Then he told everyone to wait for the dancing palm tree while he climbed up another nearby tree and hid to watch the scene.

Sure enough, along came Tortoise inside his dancing tree, unaware of what was going on. As usual everyone fled in fear, leaving Sigidi standing alone in the market. Tortoise stopped singing and looked out of the hollow tree. He couldn't believe his eyes. One man dared to stand there, seemingly unafraid. Tortoise was worried at this stubborn man. He thought perhaps he had been found out. Perhaps he should run away before he was caught.

'After all, no god favours a lazy man,' he thought. 'But on the other hand there is no god greater than my belly, which demands that I serve it.'

So he boldly ran up to the silent figure.

'How is it you are not afraid like everyone else?' he demanded. 'Aren't you going to run away?' Sigidi, of course, did not reply, in fact he didn't move a muscle.

Angrily, Tortoise shouted at him, 'Answer me, or I shall beat you.'

When Sigidi still remained silent and motionless, Tortoise slapped him hard on his face. But his paw stuck fast to the wooden image.

'Let me go,' shouted Tortoise, 'or I shall strike you with my other paw.' But Sigidi did nothing.

So Tortoise hit him with his other paw, and that stuck fast. Then in panic he kicked Sigidi, first with one foot, then the other. Now all four of his limbs were stuck and, struggle as he might, he could not get free.

'Please let me go,' cried Tortoise, 'I'm sorry. I shan't be greedy again.'

The wise old man in the tree had seen everything. Down he came from his hiding place. 'Well Tortoise, you have given these people a lot of trouble. But I've caught you now.'

Then he called the king and the people to come and see what he had found. They all crowded round Tortoise in astonishment, while the wise old man explained to them everything that had happened, including how Tortoise had hidden inside the tree.

When they heard the story everyone was very angry with Tortoise and demanded that he be punished. So the king decreed that he should be banished from the village.

The old palm tree remained in the middle of the marketplace, where it took root, and where children still gather to hear the story of the time it danced through the village. And to this day Tortoise has lived in the bush and never dares show his face among the people.

How Tortoise Grew a Tail

Unusually, in this Yoruba tale the tortoise is not in the wrong, but is himself offended against.

Once Ijapa the tortoise went on a long journey under the hot sun. After walking for many hours he was worn out, hot and hungry. Just then he reached the house of his friend Ojola, the boa. He went to his door and called to him, thinking he might get something to eat. Ojola, seeing that he was hot and tired, invited him in.

'Come in, Ijapa, and rest awhile. You are hot and tired. Why don't you wash yourself and then sit down and make yourself comfortable and get cool.'

So Ijapa came in and they sat down together to talk. But Ojola's wife was cooking, and the tortoise could smell the beautiful aroma from the pot. He began to groan with hunger.

'Does the smell of my cooking bother you?' asked the boa.

'No, it just reminds me of home, where I would be now, eating a lovely supper cooked by my wife,' replied Ijapa.

'Then let's eat together,' said Ojola. 'You go and wash and all will be ready.'

So Ijapa went out the back to wash in the stream. Feeling refreshed he came back inside to find that a large bowl of hot steaming vegetables and corn was already set down in the middle of the floor.

'Mmm!' he said licking his lips, 'That smells good.'

'Just come here and help yourself,' said Ojola, wrapping himself round the bowl and eagerly beginning to eat.

The tortoise, seeing the boa's long coils wrapped around the bowl, walked around to the other side to find a way in. But on all sides Ojola's big fat coils were piled up around the food while he slurped and supped.

'This is delicious,' said Ojola. 'What are you waiting for, Ijapa? Do join me before it all vanishes.'

'Yes I would like to join you, Ojola, but why do you wrap yourself round the food like that? I can't get at it.'

'This is our custom,' said the boa. 'We always eat our food like this, lying round it. Do come quickly and have some.'

Poor Ijapa scuttled this way and that and couldn't find a way in. Eventually he gave up just as Ojola swallowed the last mouthful.

'Well it is nice to eat with friends,' said Ojola. 'We must do this again.'

The tortoise didn't complain, but he left Ojola's house in a bad mood and more hungry than ever. Eventually he got home and brooded over what had happened. He wanted to teach the boa a lesson, so he decided to invite him over to his own house for the next festival day to return his hospitality.

While Ijapa's wife prepared a special festival meal, he busied himself weaving a tail out of grass. When it was finished he stuck it on himself with tree-gum, so that he looked as if he had grown a long, fat tail.

When Ojola arrived the tortoise greeted him at the door and invited him in.

'Come in, Ojola, and make yourself comfortable.'

So the boa came in and they sat down together to talk. Ojola could smell the beautiful aroma from the cooking and began to lick his lips.

'That cooking smells good, Ijapa. When are we going to eat?'

'Let's eat right away,' said the tortoise. 'You go and wash and all will be ready.'

So Ojola went out to the spring to wash. Feeling refreshed he came back inside to find that a big feast was laid out in the middle of the floor.

'Mmm!' he said licking his lips. 'That smells good.'

'Just come here and help yourself,' said Ijapa, as he circled round and round the food until his fat tail surrounded it on all sides. Then he began to eat.

Ojola, seeing the tortoise's strange new tail wrapped around the food, slithered round to the other side to find a way in. But on all sides Ijapa's big fat tail was piled up around the food while he slurped and supped.

'This is delicious,' said Ijapa. 'What are you waiting for, Ojola? Good food doesn't last long in this house. Do join me before it all vanishes.'

'Yes I would like to join you, Ijapa, but where did you get this big new tail of yours from? Before you were short, but now you are very long, and your tail is in my way.'

'One learns about such things from one's friends,' replied the tortoise.

Then Ojola remembered how when Ijapa had been his guest he had wrapped his tail round his food and prevented him from eating. He was ashamed and went away. From that day comes the proverb:

We learn from our friends to be short
And we also learn to be tall

Tortoise Swears an Oath

(Yoruba)

The storage house in this story stood on stilts to keep it off the ground. Hence Tortoise's wife had to stand on his shoulders to reach into it. Nevertheless, here we see Tortoise reveal his dishonest, greedy and cunning nature. This time he gets away with it, but in other stories he meets his end.

Tortoise was not the most hard-working of fellows, nor was his wife. He spent all day lazing around, and she spent her time gossiping with her friends at the market, or by the stream where they washed clothes. Between them they didn't tend their vegetable garden properly, and so they were never able to put by any food in case of hard times.

A drought fell on the country and everywhere the fields were empty. Most of the people had put aside stores for just such a time as this, but not Tortoise and his wife. They went from one to another of their friends asking for help, but none of them were able to spare any food, because they were all using their emergency supplies themselves. At last Tortoise and his wife sat down in despair, faced with hunger.

Now it happened that their next-door neighbour had been very diligent in storing up a good supply of yams.

'Our neighbour's storage house is full of yams,' said Tortoise. 'It's not right that he has so many yams while we are having to starve.'

So they made a plan. Early the next morning they took a large basket and went outside. Looking around to check that no one could see them, Tortoise spoke to his wife.

'Climb up on my shoulders.' She climbed up and sat on his shoulders. 'Now take this.' Tortoise passed up to her the large basket which she balanced on her head. Together they made their way over to their neighbour's storage house. The storage house was designed so that the yams were stored high up, out of reach of the damp ground and prying animals.

'See if you can reach the yams,' said Tortoise to his wife. She found that she was able to reach them. As quickly as she could she filled the basket on her head with yams. Then they made their way back to their house and emptied it there, her still sitting on his shoulders. Three times they filled the basket and carried the yams back to their home, until they had a pile of yams large enough to feed them for several weeks. Then they sat down feeling well pleased with themselves.

Later that morning, when their neighbour went down to his storage house to get some yams, he immediately noticed that some were missing. He looked around to see what could have happened and noticed footprints leading from his storage house all the way to the house of Tortoise and his wife. He knew about their lazy ways, and was in no doubt that it must be they who had stolen his yams. So he took them before the king and accused them of the theft.

'We are innocent,' protested the couple. 'We would never steal yams from our neighbour.'

It was the custom in those parts to test a person's innocence by a special ceremony. The accused would be taken to a local shrine where they would be invited to admit their guilt or swear their innocence. If they confessed, they would be punished according to the local law. If they claimed to be innocent they were made to drink a special herb drink called agbo. If their oath were true, after drinking the agbo they would suffer no ill effects, but if it were false, they would fall sick, and everyone would know that they were guilty.

So the king ordered that Tortoise and his wife should be taken to the shrine to drink agbo. When they arrived at the shrine all the village came out to see what would happen. Tortoise went first.

'I swear that I never raised my arms to steal the yams from my neighbour's storage house,' swore Tortoise. 'If I am lying may I fall sick and die.' Then his wife came forward.

'I swear that I never used my legs to walk up and steal the yams from my neighbour's storage house,' she swore. 'If I am lying may I fall sick and die.' The priest then gave them both a large bowl of agbo to drink. They drank every drop of agbo and everyone watched eagerly to see what would happen. Nothing happened. They were both fine.

'Release them,' ordered the king. 'They are telling the truth.' And so Tortoise and his wife got away with yet another of their mischievous deeds.

Tortoise and Babarinsa's Daughters

(Yoruba)
Again, Tortoise deceitfully gets his way, but this time he is disappointed and brings pain to others by his selfishness.

There was once a man called Babarinsa who lived in a small village. He and his wife were poor but they had three daughters who were so beautiful that every man wanted to marry them. But no matter who asked him for his daughters, whether they be rich or poor, Babarinsa would always say the same thing.

'Whoever can declare the names of my daughters in public can have all three as wives, no matter what their wealth or social position.'

He was quite sure that no one would ever learn his daughter's names. He and his wife would never call them by name outside their garden or house and they had no close neighbours. Not even the king himself could find out their names.

When Tortoise heard of Babarinsa's proclamation, he decided that he would learn the names of the beautiful daughters. First he found out where they lived with their father and then he hid himself outside the garden and watched. He watched for days and days, learning their habits and gradually coming up with a plan.

He had seen that the three daughters played in the garden every evening at sunset and so one evening he waited in a tree with three bunches of flowers. He dropped one right next to one of the sisters. Seeing the strange and beautiful flowers, she called to the other two.

'Opobipobi, Oripolobi, come here. Look at these wonderful flowers.'

Tortoise then dropped another bunch next to one of the remaining two daughters. She too called to her sisters.

'Come and see these flowers, Ajobikobi, Oripolobi.'

When Tortoise dropped his last bunch by the third girl she also called to her sisters.

'Ajobikobi, Opobipobi, I have some flowers here as well.'

And so Tortoise not only learnt all their names, but he also found out what each daughter was called. He stayed in the tree until the girls had left and then climbed down.

The next day he went to the king and told him that he had found out the names of Babarinsa's daughters and it was time to call a public meeting. The king was about to throw Tortoise out but then he remembered that Tortoise was supposed to be very clever.

'But,' replied the king, 'even if you do know their names how can you expect them to marry you. Please give their names to me instead. I will give you anything you ask for in exchange for the names.'

But Tortoise was not to be persuaded. The king became angry and, hoping that Tortoise did not really know the names, he arranged a date when anyone who wanted to, could try and win the daughters' hands in marriage.

Soon the day arrived and everyone came. They all wanted to see who, if anybody, would marry the three beautiful sisters. Finally the king announced that if anyone wanted to, they could now try their luck with the names. There was complete silence until Tortoise stepped forward. Most people just laughed but there were a few who knew how clever he was and waited in silence.

Tortoise walked over to the king, bowed and then said, 'I am very happy to be here and let me assure you that this is not a joke. I do know the names of Babarinsa's daughters and I am now ready to announce them. The first daughter,' he said as he pointed to one of the girls, 'is called Ajobikobi, the second is Opobipobi and the name of the third is Oripolobi.'

A hush fell on the crowd as the king asked Babarinsa if this was correct.

'Yes, it is,' replied an astonished and downcast Babarinsa. A happy Tortoise wasted no time in leading his new wives out of the assembly and to his own home.

Along the way the daughters discussed mournfully amongst themselves how their father had turned down the proposals of so many handsome and rich men and now they had to settle for the lowly tortoise. Finally Ajobikobi stopped by a tree and said that she would rather die than marry Tortoise. With that she turned into one of the leaves on the tree. Tortoise tried his best to find her but failed. Still, he had two other wives.

After they had gone a little further Opobipobi also stopped. She started crying and said that she too would rather lose her life than be a wife of Tortoise. Suddenly she disappeared and became one of the hundreds of ferns alongside the river bank.

Tortoise was now frightened that he may lose all three of his wives. Determined not to lose his last one, he grabbed her hand. But as soon as he touched her she turned into water and ran down to the river.

Tortoise was now stricken with grief and loneliness. He suddenly saw how proud he had been that he thought he could have such beautiful girls as wives. He ran away, deep into the forest and hid. He still hides now, afraid that if anyone sees him they will mock him and laugh at his false hopes.

Tortoise's Last Journey

One of the many painful ends of Tortoise in Yoruba stories. Osanyin, at whose shrine Tortoise is sacrificed, is the Yoruba god of medicine, who cures both physical and psychic diseases. This story explains how tortoise meat became sacred to the Osanyin cult.

Ijapa the tortoise had a guinea fowl friend called Agbe. Agbe had no land of his own, and he could neither dig nor till the soil. Whenever he was hungry he would steal a yam from the field of a certain farmer called Odi. Because he only stole one yam at a time, and was careful not to be seen, Odi suspected nothing, and Agbe was always well fed. One day Ijapa went to speak with Agbe.

'How is it that you are always well fed. I don't see you working in the fields. Where do you get your food?'

'I have a servant who works for me,' Agbe said, 'his name is Odi. He plants yams for me.'

'But you are a poor person, how can you have a servant?'

'Well, I do. He plants the yams and when they are ready I pull them up and eat them.'

'I cannot swallow your story. It has no legs to hold it up.'

So Agbe took Ijapa with him and showed him Odi's field. They stayed at the edge of the field and watched Odi working hard among the yams.

'There's my servant,' Agbe said. 'He plants, he weeds, and he takes care of my yams.'

'Then let's take some now and cook them,' said Ijapa, 'I am hungry.'

'Not now,' said Agbe, 'I have an agreement with my servant that we shall never be in the field together. Whenever he is there I stay in the bush, and when I am there he is at home sleeping. That way we don't get into arguments.'

So they waited, and at last Odi packed up his things and walked off home. Then Agbe and Ijapa went into the field and each of them pulled up a yam.

'Now let's go home,' said Agbe.

'Not yet!' protested Ijapa. 'You have a whole field full of yams, is this all you're going to offer to your guest?'

'I have an agreement with my servant,' answered Agbe, 'I only take one yam at a time.'

'How foolish and wasteful,' exclaimed Ijapa, 'and you are not at all generous.'

'All right,' said Agbe in disgust, 'Help yourself, but don't say I didn't warn you.' And he left the field and disappeared into the bush with his single yam.

Ijapa set to work without delay. He began digging up yams, as many as he could carry. He made a bundle of them and put it on his head. He made another bundle and tied it to his back. Still he was not satisfied.

'A wise man doesn't turn away from good fortune,' he said to himself. He dug up more and tied them round his neck and clutched others with his hands and feet. Then he tried to move. He could hardly walk. Slowly he dragged himself along towards the edge of the field. His load was very heavy. Eventually he got bogged down. He couldn't move another inch, but he didn't want to let go of any of the yams. He scolded the different parts of his body.

> Legs, if you don't move, no yams for you!
> Neck, if you don't pull, no yams for you!
> Back, if you don't carry, no yams for you!

But it was no good, he was completely stuck. Just then, Odi the farmer returned to his field. He saw the tortoise trying to steal away with his yams. He took the yams back, tied Ijapa up with a rope and dragged him across the field to his house. Then he picked up a big stone to kill the tortoise. But Ijapa, whose wits were sharp when he was in trouble, shouted out.

> This is not how Ijapa is killed.
> Stones cannot harm him.
> Bury him under a pile of grain instead,
> And cover him with an earthen pot.

The farmer considered what the tortoise said. Then he dropped the stone and poured a basket of millet over Ijapa, then covered him with a big pot. He left the tortoise like that for a week, then he lifted the pot to see if he was dead. To his surprise he saw that all the grain had gone, that Ijapa had got fat, and was very much alive. Ijapa laughed.

> The grain was not fierce enough to kill Ijapa.
> It couldn't subdue him.
> Better give Ijapa to a passing stranger to carry away.
> That will get rid of him!

Ijapa had been caught many times in similar situations, but he always managed to talk his way out of it. Although he was stupid in greed, when in danger he was clever. This time, however, his luck changed. The farmer listened to his words. Seeing a priest coming towards him along the path, he picked up Ijapa and handed him over to the priest.

'Priest, I am told that I should give you this.'

It so happened that the priest was on his way to the Osanyin shrine, where animals are sacrificed. A ritual was to be performed that very day and he required an animal. So he took Ijapa. And that was Ijapa's last journey.

Before that time, tortoises were never sacrificed at the shrine, but since then, because of Ijapa's clever tongue, it has become the custom to sacrifice tortoises there.

A Lesson for the Bat

(Yoruba)

One day the bat decided to visit his father-in-law. But he wanted someone to carry his drinking horn as he could not carry it at the same time as he was flying. So he asked the sheep if she could spare one of her lambs. But she told him that she did not want any of her lambs to go with him.

Then the oldest lamb interrupted, 'Mother, I have seen nothing of the world. Please let me go so I may learn something.'

And so the next day, the bat and the lamb set off. When they were about halfway there, the bat said to the lamb, 'Please hide my drinking horn in that bush so that it may be safe.'

The lamb did so and set off again happy that he no longer had to carry anything. Well past noon they arrived at the house of the bat's father-in-law. As soon as they arrived the bat told the lamb to go back and get his drinking horn. The lamb was tired out from the long journey but he went anyway.

When the lamb finally returned with the horn, the bat had already finished all the dinner and there was nothing left for the lamb.

'You were too slow,' said the bat. 'If you had been faster, there would have been some food left. Now I've already quenched my thirst with palm wine. Go back and hide the drinking horn in the bush again. But next time I ask for it make sure you are quicker.'

By the time the lamb had returned from hiding the drinking horn again, he was so tired that he went straight to sleep without even thinking about food. This was probably good because no matter how hungry he was, there was no food for him.

For the next four days the same thing happened and the lamb was getting thinner and thinner. Meanwhile the bat was getting fatter and fatter and soon he decided that it was time to go home. By the time the lamb returned to his mother, he could hardly walk. The sheep asked him what had happened and the lamb told her. The sheep was so angry that she went straight to the tortoise to ask him for advice on how to take revenge on the bat. After hearing what the bat had done to the poor lamb, the tortoise was also very angry.

'Leave everything to me,' he said. 'I will teach this bat a lesson.'

After a while the bat decided to go back to visit his father-in-law. He went back to the sheep and asked if she would let one of her lambs come with him to carry his drinking horn. But before she had time to answer, the tortoise offered to go. So the bat and the tortoise set off.

When they arrived at the bush where the lamb had hidden the drinking horn on the last trip, the bat asked the tortoise to do the same thing. But instead of leaving the horn there, he secretly put it in his bag and took it with him. When later in the day they arrived at the house, tortoise hung the drinking horn on the post at the back of the yard.

'Tortoise, it is now time to eat,' said the bat after a while. 'I will need my drinking horn. Will you go back to the bush and bring it to me?'

'With pleasure,' replied the tortoise. But he only had to go to the yard and so he was back with the horn in less than a minute. The bat was so surprised and annoyed that he would not eat. So while the bat sulked, the tortoise ate both his and the bat's portions of the very tasty food. He then returned the horn to the post at the back of the yard.

The same thing happened the next day and the next until they had been there for four days. Finally the bat could not stand the hunger any longer and asked his mother-in-law to prepare him a very large meal.

'Please don't let the tortoise see you,' he said. 'I am very tired so I will take a nap while you cook. But do it quickly for I am starving.'

But unknown to both the bat and his mother-in-law, the tortoise, who was resting in the corner, was listening to every word that they had said. The tortoise waited in the corner until the bat fell asleep and then he carried the bat into his own room. The clever tortoise then went into the bat's room and covered himself with the blanket.

Meanwhile the mother-in-law had finished cooking and left the meal in the bat's room. She saw what she thought was the bat sleeping and left. As soon as she left, the tortoise got up and ate all the food that was left there except for a small mouthful. He then drank all of the palm wine except a tiny amount. He then returned to his own room and carried the bat back into his room. Before leaving, he put the small remains of food and wine in the mouth of the bat. Before going to sleep that night, the tortoise rinsed his mouth vigorously with lots of water.

When the bat finally woke up the next day, he went straight to his mother-in-law and complained that he was still hungry because she had not given him any food.

'But I did and you ate it all last night,' she said. 'See here are the empty bowls.'

'I did not eat anything,' cried the bat. 'It must have been that tortoise.'

'Let us call everyone together and find out the truth.'

At the meeting, tortoise suggested that both he and the bat rinse their mouths with water and see whose mouth had food in it. So each rinsed their mouths and then spat out the water into two bowls. The tortoise's bowl was full of clear water but the bat's had bits of food floating in it. Both the bat's parents-in-law were disgusted with him.

'So it was you the whole time,' shouted the father-in-law. 'You have abused my wife for no reason. From now on I never want to see you again.' And with that he threw the bat out of the house.

As for the bat, he was so ashamed that he hid himself. Whenever he saw any of his family they always laughed at him because he had tried to trick his own mother-in-law. After a while he only came out at night and from that day to this, the bat always hides during the day.

How the Cat Came to Live with People

In this story from the Hausa people, the lion wrestles with and defeats the elephant, but is then himself defeated by the goat. This puts the cat's only too realistic achievement of always landing on its feet and thus avoiding being thrown and becoming the eventual winner in its true context as being an almost magical ability.

An Emir who ruled in the north of the country once decided that he would like an animal to keep him company in his palace. He sent a messenger to the animals of the bush asking them to meet and decide which animal should be chosen for this honour. They all met and discussed it. First the elephant volunteered.

'I will go and live with the Emir.'

But then the bear volunteered, then the lion, and the goat. All of them wanted to go. Tempers began to get hot.

'Let's hold a wrestling contest,' someone suggested. 'And whoever emerges undefeated will be chosen to go and live in the palace.' Everyone agreed.

The big and strong animals came forward first. The elephant wrestled with the bear and easily threw him down. Then the lion wrestled with the elephant, and managed to throw him down. The goat wrestled with the lion, and because he was so nimble, he succeeded in throwing down the lion.

At last, only the hyena remained undefeated, and the only animal who had not yet wrestled was the cat. The hyena spoke disdainfully.

'There is need for me to wrestle with the cat. He is too small and weak to be able to defeat me. I am the winner and I will go and live with the Emir in his palace.'

'No, I want to fight you,' protested the cat. 'The result is not decided until I've had my chance. We must fight.'

And so it was agreed. The two came forward to fight. They grappled and soon the hyena threw the cat across the fighting arena. But although the cat was thrown high in the air he landed on all four feet. So it was judged that he had not been properly thrown because his back had not touched the ground. The match continued and again the hyena threw the cat, and again the cat landed on his feet. The hyena became angry.

'I have thrown the cat. I have won,' he announced. But the other animals disallowed it.

'His back has not yet touched the ground,' they said.

Try as he might, although the hyena was strong and threw the cat this way and that, he couldn't throw him on his back. Somehow the cat always landed on his feet. This went on all afternoon until the sun began to sink. At last the hyena was too exhausted to continue, although the cat was still fresh. So it was agreed that the cat had won.

In triumph, the cat set off with the messenger to the palace of the Emir. When he arrived he was welcomed personally by the Emir who took him to his own private apartments where the cat was allowed to wander freely. He was given a comfortable place to sleep and was treated exactly like a member of the royal household. The cat became the intimate associate of the Emir and even during great affairs of state he was allowed to sit on his lap or rub against his legs. And so it has been ever since. The cat, who originally lived in the bush just like all the other animals, is now the privileged companion of even great rulers.

After the wrestling match, people made up a proverb about the cat:

'The cat's back never touches the ground.'

Frog Inherits the Kingdom

(Alur)

In ancient times there was a king who was getting old. He had two sons – Frog and Lizard – and had to decide which of them should inherit his kingdom. His sons were out travelling in the country, so he sent word that whichever son would arrive at the royal court first would be declared the next king. News reached the two princes, who at once made preparations for their journey. They each ground up enough corn to last them and set off on their way.

Lizard was the fastest, and he wasted no time in leaving. He didn't want to give frog a chance.

'I am far better than that ugly Frog,' he said to himself. 'Just imagine someone who travels by jumping around on his behind being made the king! I will make a far better king, and I'll make sure I get there first.' And sure enough, he was well on his way before Frog even got started.

Meanwhile Frog, who was the cleverest of the two, realized that Lizard had got a head start on him. So he thought of a plan to slow him down. Now whereas lizards like the weather to be hot and dry, frogs, as we all know, love to be out in the rain. So Frog took the branch of a certain tree, called yatkot, which had magical rain-making properties. He ground it into a powder and sprinkled the powder in water while chanting a magical incantation. Black clouds appeared in the sky and hid the sun. A strong wind began to blow, shaking the trees, and rain began to fall. Soon the rain was coming down in torrents. Frog was very happy. Off he went on his way to the king in this lovely weather – hop, hop, hop.

Meanwhile Lizard, who was far ahead, noticed the change of weather. He hated being out in the rain and thought to himself, 'I'm far ahead of Frog. I have plenty of time. Let me crawl under a rock and shelter from this nasty rain. I'll wait for it to pass, then continue, and still be sure of getting there first.' But the rain lasted for a long time.

Frog made good progress. Soon he arrived at the court, with no sign of Lizard. As he passed through the gate he told his heralds to blow their trumpets to announce his arrival. Hearing the blast of the trumpets, the king ordered all his attendants to assemble in the court and greet their Royal Prince Frog. As soon as Frog entered, all bowed to him and the king announced that he would be the one to inherit the kingdom.

Then the sun came out. Lizard crawled out from under his rock and set off at a great pace to make up for lost time. Imagine his disappointment when he finally arrived at court only to discover that Frog had already got there and had been declared the winner. Frog, magnanimous in victory, greeted Lizard.

'You may have a beautiful skin of many colours, my brother Lizard, and I may be ugly, but I'm sorry to tell you that I've won, and I will be king.'

Ever since then, when people hear the frogs croaking, they say, 'Listen to Prince Frog's heralds blowing their trumpets. Soon it will begin to rain.'

Resources

As an anthology for the general reader, this book does not carry specific bibliographical citations. We have, of course, consulted secondary literature for the Introduction. As to the tales themselves, we have made use of existing texts in English, re-arranging, modifying, or adding to the material to the degree that it suited our purposes. The publications cited below have been indispensable, in one way or another, for the outcome of this work.

Beier, Ulli. *The Origin of Life and Death*, Heinemann Educational, 1982
Cavendish, Richard. *Treasury of African Folklore: The Oral Literature, Traditions, Myths*, Marlowe & Co., 1996
Dayrell, Elphinstone. *Folk Stories from Southern Nigeria*, Greenwood Press
Knappert, Jan. 'African Religions' in *The Encyclopedia of Religion* I, ed. M. Eliade, Macmillan Reference, 1995
Knappert, Jan. *Myths and Legends of the Congo*, Nairobi, 1971
Knappert, Jan. *Kings, Gods and Spirits from African Mythology*, P. Lowe, 1986
The Aquarian Guide to African Mythology, HarperCollins, 1990
Walker, Barbara K. *The Dancing Palm Tree*, Texas, 1990

Anthologies

Arnott, Kathleen. *African Myths and Legends*, Oxford University Press, 1989

Bakare, Gbadomisi and Beier, Ulli. *Not Even God is Ripe Enough: Yoruba Myths*, Heinemann Educational, 1968

Beier, Ulli. *The Origin of Life and Death*, Heinemann Educational, 1977

Bennet, Martin. *West African Trickster Tales*, Oxford University Press, 1994

Biebuyck, Daniel P. *The Mwindo Epic from the Banyanga*, Congo Republic, University of California Press, 1972

Bleek, W.H. *Zulu Legends*, Pretoria, 1952

Callaway, Rev. Canon. *Nursery Tales, Traditions and Histories of the Zulus*, Natal, 1868

Cardinall, A.W. *Tales Told in Togoland*, Oxford, 1931

Goody, Jack. *The Myth of the Bagre*, Oxford University Press, 1972

Itayemi, P. and Gurrey, P. *Folk Tales and Fables*, Penguin Africa Series, Penguin Books, 1953

Knappert, Jan. *Myths and Legends of the Swahili*, Nairobi, 1970

Knappert, Jan. *Myths and Legends of the Congo*, Nairobi, 1970

Knappert, Jan. *Fables from Africa*, Evan Bros, 1981

Knappert, Jan. *Namibia: Land and Peoples, Myths and Fables*, Brill, 1981

Knappert, Jan. *Myths and Legends of Botswana, Lesotho and Swaziland*, Brill, 1995

Knappert, Jan. *Kings, Gods and Spirits from African Mythology*, P. Lowe, 1986

Werner, Alice. 'African Mythology', Volume 7 of *The Mythology of All Races*, Boston, 1925, pages 105–359

Werner, Alice. *Myths and Legends of the Bantu*, F. Cass, 1968

STORIES THAT CHANGE THE WORLD

Essential Chinese Mythology

MARTIN PALMER AND ZHAO XIAOMIN

From the Emperor's court to the remote mountain provinces, for centuries the storyteller has been an honoured guest in China. Some of the legends belong to a time before history was recorded, when the mythical early emperors brought the gifts of civilization to China; they reveal how mountains were formed, rivers controlled and humans created. Others come from the great historic dynasties and range from tales of famous heroes to the adventures of the ordinary peasant.

These tales are woven throughout with the folk traditions of Buddhism, Taoism and Confucianism: the adventures of Monkey reflect the arrival of Buddhism and its clash with Taoism; the magic and humour of the Eight Immortals enliven the later folk myths; the Confucian stories centre on the trials of the dutiful son. The authors draw on a selection of these myths to present a comprehensive, colourful taste of the broad tradition that informs Chinese storytelling.

Martin Palmer and Zhao Xiaomin have translated many classic poets and popular texts, including *The Illustrated Tao Te Ching*, *Kuan Yin: Myths and Prophecies* and *Travels Through Saved China*. They are currently working with Chinese Taoist communities to preserve the Sacred Mountains of China. They are both members of Icorec.

STORIES THAT CHANGE THE WORLD

Essential Russian Mythology

PYOTR SIMONOV

The variety and colour of Russian myths are as wide-ranging as the country of Russia itself. Legends tell of the arrival many centuries ago of the first Slavs, who formed close bonds with the rivers and fertile land that fed and protected them. This became the Moist Earth of their myths, alive with spirits and mysterious forces that came to govern their pattern of life. As the Slavs spread through Russia, moving across unknown mountains and barren steppes, their stories were shaped by the world they saw, the spirits they sensed and the formidable heroes they encountered.

These myths are so intricately woven into the oral traditions of the people that even with the arrival of Christianity they were not lost. One legend tells how the mighty Prince Vladimir wiped out the old gods in person, but could not wipe them out from the memory of the people. Their wonders and deeds live on in the new faith through the epic tales and folklore which are retold here.

Pyotr Simonov has travelled extensively throughout Russia and Eastern Europe. A Byzantine scholar, he is particularly interested in the links between traditional Russian culture and ecology, and is currently working on ways to revive traditional methods of farming in Russia. He is a member of Icorec.

STORIES THAT CHANGE THE WORLD

Essential Celtic Mythology

LINDSAY CLARKE

Celtic legends, with their romance and violent struggles, capture the spirit of the ancient Celts of Ireland and Wales. These tales of mighty battles fought by warrior kings, of events that trace the rise and fall of kingdoms, are rich with the magic and mystery that is woven into the lives of their people.

Reaching back to a time when the people of the Earth-goddess Danu ruled Ireland, these oral tales handed down through generations tell of the land and of remote tribes conquered by the Celts. They tell of painful battles against the giants of the deep sea, the Fomors; of the magic power of spells, the tricks of hidden spirits and leprechauns; the awesome temperament of the natural world; the power and enchantment of love and revenge. Recounted here by Lindsay Clarke, these myths draw the reader into the world of the Celts, and their history and traditions that have resonated through the ages to the present day.

Lindsay Clarke, author of *Chymical Wedding* and *Alice's Masque* and winner of the 1989 Whitbread Prize for Fiction, is one of Britain's best known novelists. He has extensive knowledge of mythology and legend and runs workshops in the UK and abroad.

Essential Celtic Mythology	1 85538 477 9	£6.99	☐
Essential Chinese Mythology	1 85538 476 0	£6.99	☐
Essential Russian Mythology	1 85538 475 2	£6.99	☐

All these books are available from your local bookseller or can be ordered direct from the publishers.

To order direct just tick the titles you want and fill in the form below:

Name: _____

Address: _____

_____

_____

Postcode: _____

Send to: Thorsons Mail Order, Dept 3, HarperCollins*Publishers*, Westerhill Road, Bishopbriggs, Glasgow G64 2QT.

Please enclose a cheque or postal order or your authority to debit your Visa/Access account —

Credit card no: _____

Expiry date: _____

Signature: _____

— up to the value of the cover price plus:

UK & BFPO: Add £1.00 for the first book and 25p for each additional book ordered.

Overseas orders including Eire: Please add £2.95 service charge. Books will be sent by surface mail but quotes for airmail dispatches will be given on request.

24-HOUR TELEPHONE ORDERING SERVICE FOR ACCESS / VISA CARDHOLDERS — TEL: 0141 772 2281